THE TENNESSEE
Divorce Client's Handbook:

What Every Divorcing Spouse Needs to Know

THE TENNESSEE
Divorce Client's Handbook:

What Every Divorcing Spouse Needs to Know

MILES MASON, SR.

MemphisDivorce.com

WORD ASSOCIATION PUBLISHERS
www.wordassociation.com
1.800.827.7903

ISBN: 978-1-59571-837-2

Designed and published by

Word Association Publishers
205 Fifth Avenue
Tarentum, Pennsylvania 15084

www.wordassociation.com
1.800.827.7903

Table of Contents

Acknowledgments

To James J. Webb, Esq., my favorite lawyer and editor. Your patience knows no limits.

To Lynn Massey, Patrick Jones, Kelly Nanney, Jessica E. Bradley, Nicole Burton, Matthew G. Washburn, and M. Taylor Oaks for contributions, research, editing, and encouragement.

To Charles R. Hofheimer, Esq., Virginia family lawyer extraordinaire, who challenged and inspired me to write this book along with Lee Rosen, North Carolina; Rich Harris, Denver; Scott David Stewart, Arizona; Marvin Solomiany and Randy Kessler, Atlanta; Kristen Hofheimer, Virginia; and Lisa Gelman, Ontario and Toronto.

To the late Presiding Judge Joe B. Jones for being my mentor, father-in-law, and my inspiration for authoring law books. We miss you. To Glenda, for not giving up on her son-in-law.

To Mom and Dad, we all miss you. Go Vols. Roll Tide. To R. Bruce Thompson, Alan G. Crone, James C. McWillie, Frank M. Mason, Patrick B. Mason, Judge John P. Colton, Jr., Barbara Price, Z. Chris Mercer, and W. Robert Vance for their friendship, professional contributions through the years, and unyielding support on many different levels.

To my guys at "the corner," who support me with questions about the impending movie productions of my books with a remarkably sincere feigned interest including but not limited to Daryl, Jason, Ken, Neil, Allan, Bob, Larry, John, Joe, and Marshall.

To my children, Anne, Miles Jr., and Abigail, my joy. Most of all, always and forever, to my wife, Sharon, who never believed me for a second when I emphatically proclaimed I would never write another book.

1
Getting Started

"Like many of life's great adventures, divorce requires one step at time. Thoughtful preparation transforms baby steps into serious, positive momentum forward."

—*Miles Mason, Sr.*

Divorce is awful. No one files for divorce on a whim. Sometimes the decision to divorce is made by one spouse, which ends up being a wake-up call for the other. Yes, reconciliation can and does occur after divorces have been filed. Some ex-spouses even remarry each other after their divorces have been granted. In addition, many marriages have been saved when couples undergo counseling with their pastors, priests, rabbis, or family therapists. To save a marriage, though, both spouses must be seriously committed to doing so.

The only good thing about divorce for most people is that it eventually ends, and life goes on for both. Always remember that the legal aspects and the emotional aspects of divorce are different matters. Quality of life after divorce is an individual choice. Three words commonly associated with divorce are "failure," "guilt," and "fear." The feelings of failure and guilt pass with time. And the fear one can feel at the thought of going through a divorce can be greatly lessened by simply learning about divorce and thereby reducing fear of the unknown. Learning begins the process of growth and change.

This book is a great first step if you are contemplating divorce. Now is the time to begin thoughtful planning. By learning about the legal aspects of divorce you'll protect yourself by knowing what's ahead before it happens and hopefully avoid impulsive and unwise decisions.

The beginning of the divorce process is the time to start setting specific goals. At first you may have just some vague ideas, but over time you will begin to know what you want for yourself and your children.

Every case is different. There is no such thing as a "standard" divorce, and law changes over time. This book was published in 2012, so if you're reading this after that year, keep in mind that the law may have changed on some points, and they could be critical points for your case. This book does not begin to address everything about divorce law; it's a first step and companion to MemphisDivorce.com, its blog, and the many instructional videos designed to give you the information you need to get started.

Keep in mind as well that the lessons here make up only half the solution. To make your way safely through the many challenges ahead, you'll need a support group of passionate, understanding family law professionals on your side. You need people who appreciate the magnitude of your troubles and can create a safe haven while you take steps to improve your life. Read. Learn. Share. Repeat. One step at a time your lawyer can help you handcraft solutions to your particular problems.

Who Stays? Who Goes?

Leaving the home is a huge step. It requires careful analysis. Rational thought, not emotional impulse, will lead to the best plan.

—*Lee Rosen,*
President, Rosen Law Firm, North Carolina

If you don't want to leave the marital residence, don't be bullied into doing so. Don't feel you must leave just because your spouse asks you to.

Regardless, though, always put your immediate safety and that of your children first. If you feel threatened by your spouse, call the police. Ask the police or your pastor, priest, or rabbi for a referral to a shelter. Talk to a lawyer. Learn whether you should apply for an order of protection that prevents your spouse from coming around you and the children. An order of protection can provide other protection too, including legally preventing your spouse from carrying a gun.

Leaving home may reduce your stress today, but it may result in additional stress later, so it's critical if you're thinking about leaving your marital residence that you talk to your lawyer first. Consider the increase in costs and the stress that could result. If you leave, you may be required to pay your share of household expenses for the marital residence even though you're no longer living there. Living together offers a unique opportunity to share expenses more efficiently. Thus when one spouse leaves, where there was once only one mortgage, one power and gas bill, one cable bill, one bill for Internet access, and one set of appliances, there will then be need for two sets of these and other basics and the bills that come along with. Many judges feel that separation is not an excuse for leaving bills unpaid. The departing spouse may be required to contribute to paying bills incurred at the marital residence if the spouse who stayed can't afford all the expenses alone.

In addition, if you leave the marital residence while the divorce is pending, there can be unresolved legal issues. What parenting time will the parent not living with the child or children have? If the departing parent's new residence is unsuitable for overnight parenting, that might cause a greatly reduced parenting schedule. Later, courts will look to determine if the status quo is working when considering awarding parenting time in the final decree. That means that during the divorce both parents need to orchestrate parenting time so that it's as close to their preferred situation as quickly as possible. Many experienced family lawyers advise clients to resolve as many legal issues as possible before moving out.

Make sure you get copies of every document you can before you leave. You'll find a list of specific documents in chapter 12 of this book. But if you can't find particular files, at least try to make sure you write down account numbers. Keep all the documents and information safe.

If you don't want to leave, can you force your spouse to leave? Tennessee law considers kicking a spouse out of his or her home a very drastic action. In most cases, unless there has been domestic violence, neither spouse can force the other to leave. There may, however, be exceptions based on your individual situation and your judge. Some judges have ordered spouses to leave their residences without evidence of domestic violence, but that's unusual.

If you must stay in the same residence during the divorce process, be smart, stay calm, and protect yourself. Try to sleep in a room separate from your spouse. Stop living like you once did. Don't cook for the other. Don't be romantic or send mixed signals. Do your own laundry. Get your own cell phone, separate from the family plan, to prevent your spouse from tracking your calls. Keep all your divorce information safe, even if that means keeping it somewhere else. If you think your divorce will be hotly contested, assume everything you do or say will be digitally recorded. It just might be.

Whether you stay or go, immediately change all your online usernames and passwords for all bank accounts and personal communications. Create a new e-mail account for communicating with your lawyer. Use Gmail or Hotmail so you can check your e-mail from different locations. Get off or turn off your Facebook and other social media that can be used to track your activities and communications. Your social media postings can be used as evidence against you no matter what you say or why you say it. Lawyers are experts at twisting words.

This is an important time also to maintain or regain contact with significant people in your life. Make a complete list of telephone numbers, addresses, and e-mails of preachers or priests or rabbis, doctors, teachers, dentists, financial advisors,

CPAs, counselors, insurance agents, stockbrokers, day care centers, and employers as well as family and friends. Let people who care about you know what's going on. Even if you don't know what to say, let them know how you're doing, and don't be afraid to ask for help. Talking with your closest friends and family is sometimes exactly what you'll need the most.

Don't have sexual relations with your spouse, especially if your spouse has cheated on you. In legal terms, cheating is adultery. Adultery is a ground, or legal basis, for divorce. Also, adultery may be considered by the courts as marital fault, one of the factors for alimony. Once you have marital relations with your spouse after learning about his or her cheating, you may be forgiving your spouse. This is "condonation," and it's a defense to a divorce on the grounds of adultery. Plus, having relations with your spouse may send mixed signals.

Financial Planning

There is no one way to handle every divorce situation, but consider these simple strategic financial moves:

- Open a bank account to which only you have access. Deposit your earnings in that account, but understand that earnings deposited in a separate account are still considered marital property.
- If you receive automatic deposits from any source, have them deposited in your new account.
- If you pay bills by automatic withdrawal, deal with how those bills will get paid after you make changes to accounts.

- Maximize cash assets in your individual name. You need to prepare to be responsible for your own legal fees, expert fees, and courts costs in addition to other living expenses.
- Consider requesting a credit limit increase on credit cards and lines of credit—just in case.
- If your mail is not absolutely secure, obtain a post office box for bills and correspondence from your lawyer.
- If a divorce has been filed, learn if a mandatory injunction has been issued and how that may affect you. (See discussion of "Mandatory Injunction" below.) Check with your lawyer before transferring money between accounts.
- Talk to your lawyer to see how much of the joint funds you can move. Prior to issuance of the mandatory injunction, it may make sense to move half the balances from joint checking accounts, joint savings accounts, and joint investments into your own accounts.
- Run your own credit report and read it in detail. Look for previously unknown debt obligations.
- Cancel joint credit card accounts. This reduces the risk of your spouse increasing joint debt.
- Make hard copies of account statements and key documents.
- Determine if you need a financial advisor separate from your spouse's. There are many financial advisors willing to help, and even if you don't have that much in assets, a financial advisor can help you take care of what you have. Ask your family lawyer for a referral.

- If you need temporary support, you can file for divorce and ask the court to order your spouse to pay it. This is called *pendente lite* support, and it can include temporary alimony, child support, and attorney's fees.
- If you and your spouse executed wills together and signed durable powers of attorney, tell your lawyer as soon as possible. Durable powers of attorney may allow your spouse to act on your behalf in many legal and financial situations. You need to revoke the power authorized in that document.

Resources

In the early period of separation, feelings are hurt, and communication can be difficult. Money may be tight for both spouses. The departing spouse may be paying rent or have a new mortgage as well as moving fees and expenses for furnishings and appliances. Negotiating for everyday living expenses is never easy, and making sure you are not at a disadvantage can be tough, but money keeps the lights on. Divorces are expensive. Resources matter.

If the departing spouse is the supported spouse, she or he may feel desperate, and this can lead to a series of poor, short-term decisions. If the departing spouse is the primary earner, he or she is in control of where paychecks get deposited and can manage cash flow, which is obviously important.

Even though most judges take a very dim view of one spouse leaving the other destitute, the unsupported spouse may need to get to court to be awarded temporary support.

Marshaling resources can help balance the power between the spouses, preventing a helpless feeling from dictating day-to-day decision making. Save money. Resist the temptation to immediately buy new things to replace the old. Ask others for used furniture, children's clothes, and toys. Stay calm. Manage the situation as best you can.

Budgeting

It is essential that you get a handle on your finances. Create a budget. Dave Ramsey's *Total Money Makeover* is a great book for help. Listen to his radio show and/or podcast, free on iTunes. Later, consider attending his Financial Peace University. To learn more about Dave Ramsey, visit www.DaveRamsey.com.

To budget, start with income. What are your sources of earned income? Are there other sources of income? What about your spouse's income? Your lawyer will need copies of documents about current income, so make copies of current pay stubs, last year's last pay stub, W-2s, bank statements, and tax returns.

Then list expenses. Be thorough. It's easy to move quickly and forget something. If you have them, make copies of personal financial reports from Quicken or QuickBooks, canceled checks, and credit card statements. The more detailed a budget you prepare, the better an understanding you'll have of your needs and resources. Later on your lawyer will help you organize things in the format your court will want to see. But for the present you need to determine how much money it takes you to live on or what you have left over to help support your spouse. Having a detailed budget will help you make smarter decisions.

Getting a divorce is not an excuse for lavish spending even if you feel entitled to or worthy of it. Most judges expect spouses to be more frugal during divorces than they might be ordinarily. Avoid the temptation to buy that new car or furniture you may have been eyeing even if you might have bought them divorce or no divorce. Expensive vacations, even with the children, may be a bad idea as well. Even though you may be tempted to claim this level of spending is appropriate, all you may be doing is creating a big credit card bill your spouse may later absolutely refuse to pay. This might put you in a position of having to go to court in an attempt to force the other spouse to pay for arguably questionable spending. Overspending can backfire; you could end up having to defend spending choices that may have been made in anger or frustration. Don't give your spouse's lawyer ammunition with which to challenge your judgment. Be conservative and frugal with your money and your choices.

Parenting Apart

A parent moving out of the marital home affects children. Some parents think it reduces stress for the children, especially if the parents are constantly arguing. In some cases it may, but the stress the children can be under is going to be high regardless. When possible, both parents should work together to help children through the transition. Change is emotionally unsettling for everyone but especially for children.

Depending on your children's ages, they may not understand what's happening. Whether moving out is the first of many changes or the last step during the divorce process, children often don't have the emotional tools to deal with divorcing parents and the fact that one parent is no longer living with them. Professional counseling can help. A qualified mental health professional can help smooth the transition and at the same time listen for warning signs of more-serious problems.

Start and keep a parenting journal and a detailed calendar. Record events, overnights spent with the children, and time the children spend with the other parent. What scheduled parenting time was missed by your spouse? What was the excuse this week? What requested parenting time was denied? Do not include flippant comments like "Jerkface failed to make Tommy's baseball game *again.*" The calendar or journal may be shown in court someday as a contemporaneous record of what happened. If there is serious conflict between the parents, this type of information is too important to risk to a faulty memory. During times of stress, memories can be especially short-lived creatures. Credibility comes with having specific knowledge of dates and circumstances and documentation to back it up. Even without any major conflict, a journal can document what went well. Recording parenting successes can be just as important as documenting failures.

As you plan, think about everyone's schedules for work, school transportation, extracurricular activities, holidays, and doctors' visits as well as the other parent's time constraints. Later, you will need to prepare a parenting plan that takes into account an entire year's parenting time, also called residential time. In addition, you need to think about who makes which decisions. In Tennessee, the parent with whom the children reside on any particular day is generally responsible for day-to-day decisions when exercising parenting time. The parents may share or alternate other final decision-making authority such as education, choice of physicians, extracurricular activities, and choice of religion. The permanent parenting plan will establish parenting time and decision-making authority.

Parenting Schedules Are Important to Get Right—Right Now

Whether or not you want to be the "primary residential parent" (formerly known in Tennessee as the "custodial parent"), you need to decide if you want to maximize the amount of parenting time and involvement you have with your children. If either parent moves out, get the desired routine in effect as soon as possible.

If the parents can't agree on a parenting schedule, either one may ask the court to adopt a temporary parenting plan. The status quo is vitally important in all family law matters because "If it ain't broke, why should I fix it?" a judge may ask. Some judges will leave a current parenting time routine in effect if the schedule is working reasonably well. Proving that the status quo is not working reasonably well can sometimes be more difficult than one would think. Later, the parents can negotiate a different schedule, or the judge may order something different, but it may be more of an uphill battle than it needs to be.

Talk with your lawyer as soon as possible about making adjustments to the parenting schedule you feel are needed. Furthermore, remember that no matter how the divorce progresses, you must do your very best every day to stay involved with your children. If you can't see them, call them, e-mail them, Skype them—do whatever it takes to keep in touch even if it's just a five-minute phone call before bed. Tell your children you love them and give them a chance to talk to you.

Dating? Really?

Dating is not a good idea. This may be the most ignored legal advice given by family lawyers to their clients. Many people start a new relationship prior to considering divorce, so is it really that big of a deal? It can be. Often the advice not to date does not change even if the other spouse has already left the marital residence and is living with another person.

Some may say to themselves, "The marriage has already fallen apart, so what's the harm?" While it's natural to want to seek affirmation from another in times of stress, don't date. Every choice you make can be subject to scrutiny by courts, especially when children are involved. Most courts treat adultery as meaning that a person has had sexual intercourse with someone other than that person's spouse—even if separated and living apart. Even if the relationship is more emotional than physical, judges may treat the two similarly. Tennessee courts can rule that the extramarital relationship can constitute inappropriate marital conduct even if there is no "hard evidence" of sexual intercourse.

Evidence of adultery can affect court decisions about custody and the amount of parenting time because affairs can negatively impact children. The paramour may even be subjected to scrutiny. A DUI, a prior drug conviction, an awkward Facebook photo, and, yes, even a bad-check arrest could end up being mentioned in court pleadings or arguments. Even if the children have never met or seen the boyfriend or girlfriend, they may learn about the relationship from a third party in a way no one wants.

Even if there is no actual harm to a child, judges are fearful of the possibility of harm, particularly psychological. Judges expect parents to make their children their highest priority. Extramarital relationships are never viewed as putting children first. The perception of priorities matters a great deal.

In addition, allowing children to interact with a paramour is a very bad idea. Children who find someone new in their lives can become confused during an already challenging time, and courts may see this exposure as evidence of very poor judgment, giving it a reason to award custody to the other parent. Parents should always be a positive role model for their children.

In addition, adultery is legal grounds for divorce. Proving adultery can often be a challenge, although many divorcing spouses admit affairs. But know that direct evidence of the affair may not be required to prove adultery. Circumstantial evidence may be enough.

Furthermore, in Tennessee, "the relative fault of the parties" is considered by courts when deciding alimony. Having an affair before or after separation can constitute marital fault. The affair may not affect the alimony determination one way or the other, but it could possibly play an important role in the decision; it just depends on the circumstances. In any event you can bet the lawyer of the spouse not having an affair will make as much noise about the affair during court proceedings as possible. That is never comfortable for the spouse having the affair.

Even when there are no children, dating is still a bad idea. Not only can dating alter the relative negotiating positions of the spouses, but affairs often inflame emotions—fueling the need to seek retribution and revenge. Money is often seen as the vehicle for both punishment and vindication. The other spouse may decide to take the deposition of the boyfriend or girlfriend and ask embarrassing questions about the first time sex occurred, gifts, loans, and trips. In other words, don't give your spouse a reason to hate you and fight you tooth and nail.

Never forget one important rule during a divorce—don't ever give a judge a reason to dislike you. Explaining an extramarital relationship is always tricky, but telling the truth is vitally important. Getting caught in a lie can be a lot worse than actually having an affair. If you lie, you can destroy your credibility, and that's never worth it. Also, know that one spouse's dating can be found out by the other spouse no matter how careful the one tries to keep it secret. Know that one spouse can ask the other about affairs under oath during the divorce—in written discovery, during a deposition, and during trial. Also, one spouse may compel the other to produce cell phone records and credit card statements that may contain damaging evidence.

If you have already started a relationship before you read this, your situation is not unusual. You are not the first, and you will certainly not be the last. But tell your lawyer. Talk it through. Don't let your lawyer find out about the relationship later from your spouse's lawyer. You'll need to make some tough decisions. You might decide to dump the relationship, or you might choose to live with the consequences. Just make sure the decisions you make are *informed* decisions.

Stress Management is Very Important

Managing stress during a divorce is more important than you might think. Stress can lead to very serious depression and poor decision making. No one can completely eliminate physical and emotional problems associated with complex legal problems such as divorce, but counseling, proper nutrition, and moderate exercise can have a very positive impact on your well-being and judgment. If you have health concerns, consult your doctor.

And don't be afraid to seek counseling. Ask your lawyer for a referral. If you have access to a mental health professional through your employer's medical plan, take advantage of it. Realize that even if things aren't bad right this second, they can become bad down the line. Have a plan. Having someone to talk to can make all the difference. If you have sought counseling in the past and you didn't like the counselor for whatever reason, try again with another counselor. It's not unusual to try more than one or two before finding one who's right for you.

Eat smart. Stay away from fats and sugar. Overeating comfort food can lead to feeling even worse physically and emotionally. Eat fruits, vegetables, and foods containing protein. Exercise in moderation. Stay hydrated. Relax. Get to bed on time, and get plenty of sleep. Even if you're having a hard time sleeping, try to avoid regularly relying on sleeping pills. Work on your divorce some every day, perhaps for an hour or two or as necessary, but then give yourself "permission" to set the matter aside and enjoy your favorite TV show or hobby, knowing that you've made progress and will do so again. This will help combat any feelings of helplessness you might have, and you will make progress. Focus on taking things one step at a time, and realize that sometimes those steps must be baby steps.

Finally, your head must be as clear as possible. Avoid stressful situations. Say no to everything you absolutely can say no to. Remember what they say on airplanes: if you're on a plane and those oxygen masks drop, put your mask on first before assisting others with theirs. If you can't breathe, you can't be expected to help with other people's problems. Now is the time for you to take care of you. If this means giving short shrift to someone—except your children, of course—you can always make it up that person later. You'll be back to being you sooner than you think.

Assemble Your Team

Hire an experienced family lawyer. See "Choosing and Working with a Lawyer," chapter 13, in this book. Making smart decisions may never have been as important as it is now. Financial advisors often can be a great help. Many will help you without significant charge, hoping you will become a client for many years to come. Private investigators, forensic accountants, or business appraisers may become important too. If you don't have people in mind, an experienced family lawyer will be able to make great referrals.

Domestic Violence

Unfortunately, family lawyers see domestic violence more regularly than most people think. This national problem knows no economic, societal, or racial boundaries. In the 1990s, Tennessee dramatically changed its civil and criminal laws to provide more legal protection for abused spouses. If you have ever been a victim of domestic violence, if you fear reprisal for filing for divorce, or even if you are the aggressor, be sure to discuss the whole matter with your lawyer. There are important legal steps you can take to help your situation.

One of these steps is getting a protective order. A protective order enjoins the parties against coming around, abusing, harassing, or threatening each other. The restrictions can also prevent one or both parties from contacting or telephoning the other. In most cases a protective order is effective. When law enforcement officers see a party violating the protective order, the violator will be arrested. If law enforcement is not present, violation of the protective order can result in a petition for contempt being filed later that seeks jail time, fines, and/or legal fees. Judges take such violations very seriously.

The person subject to a state court–issued protective order must also understand and comply with federal law prohibiting carrying firearms. There are no exceptions, even for law enforcement personnel. Ask your lawyer for more details.

If you find yourself in the middle of a domestic violence altercation, call the police first, and do so immediately. If you are represented, also call your lawyer. The law dictates that law enforcement's preferred response to domestic violence is arrest. If you fear for your life and have nowhere to go, the police may direct you to an absolutely secret shelter. At these shelters even your lawyer is not allowed to know where you are. If you have children, they may go as well.

If you are the victim of abuse, never underestimate the true danger that rage can pose. Fight any feelings you might have of responsibility for the abuse. In the middle of a difficult situation worry about one thing only—saving your life and the lives of your children. Sort out the details later.

If you are the abuser, seek treatment. You are not alone. Help is available. The cycle of rage and terror will continue without some form of professional intervention. Don't risk jail time and losing parental rights.

Costs of Divorce

If you ask an experienced divorce lawyer why divorces cost so much, most answers will mention the factors of revenge, pride, and fear. In some cases an aggrieved spouse may seek revenge by directing his or her attorney to make the process as painful and expensive as possible. In other cases a high legal price tag results because one party has been denied access to the other's accounts, which has caused the party denied access to initiate costly discovery and motion practice. Sometimes certain assets are complicated and difficult to value, as with a closely held business or professional practices, which can also increase the cost, especially if experts are required to put a value on the business or practice. (See chapter 11 for a detailed discussion of evaluating professional practices.) A spouse has the right to learn about and completely understand the other spouse's complete financial picture before determining a settlement position.

Some cases might not have a great deal of conflict, but the cost of the divorce may be driven up by the size of the estate and whether it contains complex assets. For example, a divorcing couple who have been married for five years, who rent a house, who have no pensions, and who own no businesses can expect a much lower legal bill than a couple who are married twenty-five years, have two kids in private high schools, have pensions, own a vacation home, and have stock options.

If you're worried about the cost of your divorce, discuss this with your divorce attorney. Be honest about your resources and any fears you may have. Don't avoid this discussion. There are opportunities in every case to reduce expenses. Agree to accept legal services only if you can pay for them.

Your exact legal fee will vary based on all kinds of factors. Family law cases require many services and activities. Legal issues include separation, divorce, custody, visitation, alimony, child support, property division, valuation of assets, and attorney's fees and costs. Services may include court appearances, legal research, investigation, drafting correspondence, conferences with you, settlement negotiations with your spouse's attorney, preparation of pleadings and other legal documents, pretrial discovery, mediation, trial preparation, and trial. You will also need to obtain advice concerning your assets, liabilities, income, expenses, insurance, and taxes as well as recommendations concerning property division and support. If a trial is necessary, the court has the authority to order one spouse to pay the other's legal fees in alimony, child support, and child custody matters. If there is a trial, courts rarely order the full amount of attorneys' fees be paid by the other spouse.

The most common method of calculating legal fees by far is charging for the amount of time required for each service.

Lawyer's hourly rates can differ dramatically; their hourly rates can range from $150 per hour to over $500 per hour, but a greater hourly rate does not guarantee a superior service. Some lawyers' hourly rates depend on the complexity of the case.

One method of calculating fees is establishing a flat fee, and flat fees may be charged for the entire divorce or for a particular stage of litigation.

In addition to legal fees, there are copying costs, expert witness fees, court reporter fees, mileage, and other expenses. In addition, the court clerk may charge court costs, which may be based on the number of motions or other pleadings filed. Court costs, which are in addition to the initial case filing fees, may be nothing or may amount to several hundred dollars. For more discussion about hiring lawyers and keeping costs down, see chapter 13.

Who Should File First?

In many cases it does not matter who files first. If there is a trial, the party filing first will likely get to argue first, which is often an advantage. But most cases are settled without ever going to trial. There can be important strategic reasons for waiting until the other spouse files. It depends on many different factors such as the spouses' relative anger and fault and the makeup of the estate. Unlike fine wine, legal problems do not improve with age. Two good reasons for filing for divorce first include obtaining a mandatory injunction (see below) and gaining access to a temporary support hearing. Both require a divorce to be filed.

Mandatory Injunction

Tennessee law provides for a mandatory injunction that grants the person filing the divorce (or a countercomplaint) the ability to obtain a court order preventing either party from engaging in certain potentially harmful activities, including the following:

1. (A) Each party is restrained and enjoined from transferring, assigning, borrowing against, concealing or in any way dissipating or disposing of any marital property without the consent of the other party or an order of the Court.

   (B) Expenditures from current income to maintain the marital standard of living and usual and ordinary costs of operating a business are not restricted by this injunction. Each party shall maintain records of all expenditures, copies of which shall be available to the other party upon request.

2. Each party is restrained and enjoined from voluntarily canceling, modifying, terminating, assigning, or allowing to lapse for non-payment of premiums, any insurance policy including, but not limited to life, health, disability, homeowners, renters and automobile, where such insurance policy provides coverage to either of the parties or the children, or that names either of the parties of the children as beneficiaries, without the consent of the other party or an order of the Court.

"Modifying" includes any change in beneficiary status.

3. Each party is restrained from harassing, threatening, assaulting or abusing the other and from making disparaging remarks about the other in the presence of any children of the parties or to either party's employer.

4. Each party is restrained and enjoined from hiding, destroying or spoiling, in whole or in part, any evidence electronically stored or on computer hard drives or other memory storage devices.

5. Each party is restrained from removing the children of the parties from the State of Tennessee, or more than one hundred (100) miles from the marital home, without the permission of the other party or an order of the Court, unless in the case of a removal based upon well-founded fear of physical abuse against either the fleeing parent or the child. In such cases, upon request of the non-relocating parent, the Court will conduct an expedited hearing, by phone conference, if appropriate, to determine the reasonableness of the relocation and to make such other orders as appropriate.

6. The provisions of Section 36-6-101(a)(3) shall be applicable upon fulfillment of the requirements of subsection (d) of this act. [See parental rights listed in chapter 4.]

7. This injunction shall not preclude either party from applying to the Court for further temporary orders, an expanded injunction or modifications or revocation of this temporary injunction.

8. This temporary injunction remains in effect against both parties until the Final Decree of Divorce or Order of Legal Separation is entered, the petition is dismissed, the parties reach agreement or until the Court modifies or dissolves the injunction.

Temporary Support

Once a divorce has been filed, temporary support may be awarded if the parties cannot reach an agreement regarding their bills and finances. Temporary support includes temporary alimony, child support, and attorney's fees. In some counties in Tennessee it is called filing a "motion for support *pendente lite.*" In Shelby County, the hearing occurs before a divorce referee and may be appealed to the judge or chancellor. In most counties across the state the trial judge will hear the motion. These motions are often heard in an abbreviated proceeding that may include time limitations.

Most judges will limit testimony during the temporary support hearing to financial issues, such as who makes how much money and what bills must be paid. Questions about why certain bills exist and who is at fault for the divorce take a backseat in these hearings. For these hearings, most courts want to make sure only that the bills get paid and the status quo is maintained the best it can be until the divorce is resolved.

Just because an obligor spouse, the one legally required to pay, is ordered to pay a certain amount in temporary support does not mean the same support amount will be ordered in the divorce. In fact, that is rarely the case for many reasons. The temporary order ends when the final judgment for divorce is entered.

Before or after the divorce is filed, the parties can attend mediation if they both agree to it, or the parties can agree to participate in a collaborative law process. Both these processes are discussed in more detail in chapter 7. The key to both processes resulting in a settlement depends on the willingness of both parties to share in a timely manner all the needed financial information and cooperate with each other as much as possible.

Read this entire book. It includes the basics of what every person going through a divorce in Tennessee really needs to know. From there you'll be able to ask your lawyer intelligent questions. After you get your answers, you'll be better able to make decisions. Remember that there are always exceptions to what is said here. In no way should the material in this book substitute for competent legal advice from an experienced family lawyer.

To learn more about complicated divorce issues involving self-employed professionals and business owners or the proper handling of a divorce case using a forensic accountant, consider purchasing *The Forensic Accounting Deskbook: A Practical Guide to Financial Investigation and Analysis for Family Lawyers*, published by the American Bar Association Family Law Section and written by Miles Mason, Sr. For more information about that book see www.ForensicAccountingDeskbook.com or www.MemphisDivorce.com.

2
Tennessee Divorce Law and Procedure

To fight and conquer in all our battles is not supreme excellence;
supreme excellence consists in breaking the enemy's resistance
without fighting.

—Sun Tzu, Chinese military strategist

The task at hand is gaining knowledge of Tennessee divorce law and procedure. Learning reduces anxiety and fear of the unknown. In this chapter you'll find terms and concepts that will help you better understand how everything interrelates. While the rest of the book describes the details of property division, alimony, child custody, child support, and other important issues—your destination, this particular chapter describes the road you'll take to get there.

There are only two ways to end a marriage: a divorce trial or a settlement. Almost everyone agrees that a settlement is less traumatic and does less damage to everyone involved, especially children. Settlements definitely cost less than trials, and very few divorces these days actually end in trials. Before a settlement is reached or a trial is held, however, the divorce process begins.

Tennessee's laws governing divorce are found in chapter 36 of the Tennessee Code, which are called statutes, and in opinions handed down by the Supreme Court of Tennessee and Court of Appeals. Each state has its own laws, which can vary substantially. Statutes can be hard to read, and each judge could interpret or apply these laws differently just because every case is different. Trying to figure out and explain how a particular law might be applied in a given person's situation is what lawyers do for a living. Practicing family law is part art and part science.

Complaint for Divorce

The complaint for divorce and request for relief that the complaint includes generally ask the court to divide property, order alimony and child support, and provide for everything else possible. A court cannot grant relief that is not requested. A complaint for divorce that asks for everything does not necessarily mean there's going to be a full-scale war because most cases settle. Experienced family law attorneys will advise their clients to prepare for trial but always allow for a settlement opportunity if and when it arises. So if the primary breadwinner asks for custody of the children, child support, and alimony, that does not necessarily really mean that spouse actually expects to receive custody, child support, and alimony.

According to Tennessee law, a spouse must be a resident within Tennessee for at least six months prior to filing for divorce, or the acts complained of in the complaint for divorce must have occurred in Tennessee. Some exceptions may apply for emergency situations such as serious child or spousal abuse. Battles over which state has jurisdiction over children can be complicated and very expensive. Custody battles contested in more than one state usually require judges from both states to communicate and decide which state will hear the case. Most states have adopted a very complicated law called the Uniform Child Custody Jurisdiction and Enforcement Act. One of the key factors is which state is the "home state" of the children, which usually means where the children lived six months prior to the filing for divorce.

Cases are most often filed in the county where the parties last lived together. If neither is still living in that county, the case will most likely be filed where the filing party lives at the time. This is called venue.

Most lawyers will include within the divorce complaint certain allegations and requests for relief from the court that may or may not have a likelihood of success. If a certain matter is not listed, the court may not have the authority to grant the relief. At the beginning of the case, lawyers can't know what may happen in the future. So the safest tactic is to ask for every possible type of relief in the complaint. This is not an attempt to intimidate or embarrass the other party publicly but a routine practice. For example, a parent who files for divorce may not realistically be seeking custody of a child but may still request in the complaint for divorce that a child support payment be paid by the other parent.

The complaint for divorce comprises several sections:

1. **Caption:** The caption, which heads off all legal pleadings, lists the names of the parties, the title of the court in which the action is being heard, the docket number, and the title of the pleading. In the complaint it will most likely read "Complaint for Divorce" or "Petition for Divorce."

2. **Petitioner's Statement Under Oath:** A complete list of statistical information is mandatory in the complaint, including the basis for jurisdiction, identifying information of the parties and any children of the parties, the date and place of the marriage, the grounds for divorce, certain custody information, descriptions of real property, and other facts that may be unique or relevant to the relief requested from the court.

3. **Prayer for Relief:** The person filing the pleading normally asks the court to grant everything imaginable, including property division, receipt of alimony, custody, child support, temporary support, and any other relief. This is normal even if the person asking for the relief is the primary breadwinner.

4. **Signature of the Party:** The party signing the petition states that the information is correct to the best of that person's information, knowledge, and belief.

5. **Signature of the Attorney:** When an attorney signs a pleading, the attorney is certifying that

the information is correct and not filed for an improper purpose.

Serving the divorce papers means actually delivering the summons (official notice of the lawsuit) and complaint for divorce to the other party. The other spouse's lawyer, if known, may accept service, but most attorneys have a process server actually hand the paperwork to the other spouse. The process server can be a sheriff's deputy or a private process server. Sheriff's deputies have an annoying habit of knocking on doors as early as 4:30 a.m. Under certain circumstances you may be able to mail copies to your spouse's residence, or if you don't know where your spouse is, you may publish a legal notice in a newspaper. Personal service of the divorce complaint and summons is preferred.

The cost of filing for divorce depends on the county. Some are more expensive than others. In Shelby County, Tennessee, for instance, the cost may be over $300.

Grounds for Divorce

Grounds for divorce must be alleged and either proven or agreed upon by the parties. In the vast majority of settlements, one (possibly both) of the spouses will be granted a divorce on the grounds of "irreconcilable differences." Only one ground must be proven or agreed upon. Most divorces allege no-fault grounds, irreconcilable differences, and fault grounds, most often "inappropriate marital conduct" (formally known as cruel and inhuman treatment). Even though a complaint may contain an allegation of inappropriate marital conduct, that does not mean that fault will become a central issue in the case or that the granting of a divorce will be contested.

Grounds and fault are two separate legal issues. Fault is a factor for alimony determinations. The same acts or series of acts, say adultery, can serve both as grounds for divorce and fault for determination of alimony. This is one of the most important reasons you should share with your lawyer the worst thing your spouse may claim you have done even if it's not true. From the very beginning, it is important to be able to defend against a claim for grounds or provide an explanation why the act was reasonable or justified.

Most judges interpret the meaning of inappropriate marital conduct very broadly. Inappropriate marital conduct is the willful, persistent causing of unnecessary suffering whether by realization or apprehension, whether of the mind or body, in such a way as to render cohabitation unsafe and unendurable. It is not restricted to physical injury but includes such willful and persistent conduct that endangers the offended spouse's physical and/or mental health. Examples of inappropriate marital conduct include spreading false accusations of adultery, abnormal sexual behavior, browbeating and bullying, attentions to persons of the opposite sex, the use of profanity toward the spouse, failure to provide a suitable home and clothing, holding a gun on the spouse, notice to merchants not to extend credit to the spouse, and making threatening telephone calls. A combination of lesser acts over a period of time, when joined together, may constitute inappropriate marital conduct.

If your spouse does not want a divorce (for vindictive or other reasons) and there may be lack of proof of bad acts committed by your spouse, grounds could become an important issue. But that is rare these days. Discuss your situation with your lawyer. Other grounds for divorce under Tennessee law include:

- Either party, at the time of the contract, was and still is naturally impotent and incapable of procreation;
- Either party has knowingly entered into a second marriage when he or she was still married to someone else;
- Either party has committed adultery;
- Willful or malicious desertion or absence of either party without a reasonable cause for one whole year;
- Being convicted of any crime that by the laws of the state renders the party infamous;
- Being convicted of a crime that by the laws of the state is declared to be a felony, and being sentenced to confinement in the penitentiary;
- Either party has attempted the life of the other by poison or any other means showing malice;
- Refusal on the part of a spouse to remove with that person's spouse to this state without a reasonable cause and being willfully absent from the spouse residing in Tennessee for two years;
- The wife was pregnant at the time of the marriage by another person without the knowledge of the husband;
- Habitual drunkenness or abuse of narcotics by either party when the spouse has contracted either such habit after marriage;
- Irreconcilable differences between the parties;

- For a continuous period of two or more years that commenced prior to or after April 18, 1985, both parties have lived in separate residences, the parties have not cohabitated as man and wife during such period, and there are no minor children of the parties;
- The husband has offered such indignities to the wife's person as to render the wife's condition intolerable and thereby forced the wife to withdraw; and
- The husband has abandoned the wife or turned the wife out of doors and refused or neglected to provide for the wife.

Defenses

There are a number of defenses to grounds for divorce as well. When a spouse files for divorce in Tennessee, the opposing spouse is given the opportunity to raise an argument in his or her defense. These are called "affirmative defenses" because they admit that the alleged misconduct occurred. Affirmative defenses provide a valid reason for the spouse to have committed the misconduct. In other words, an affirmative defense is raised as a justification or excuse for marital wrongdoing. Tennessee recognizes affirmative defenses to both adultery and inappropriate marital conduct.

There are three affirmative defenses to adultery under Tennessee statute:

1. Recrimination. Let's suppose a wife engages in an extramarital affair. The husband finds out about the affair and files for divorce. The wife should raise an affirmative defense of "recrimination" if she can prove that the husband is also guilty of adultery. If recrimination is established, neither the husband nor the wife may use adultery as grounds for divorce. In this situation one of the parties must find an alternate grounds for divorce before the court will grant a decree.

2. Condonation. The premise of this defense is that the nonoffending spouse has in some manner "condoned" the misconduct. As an example, suppose the wife is in an extramarital affair but the husband is not. The husband finds out about the affair and does not file for divorce. A number of years later the husband files for divorce on the grounds of adultery. The wife could raise the affirmative defense of condonation. This defense is valid only if the husband knew the full extent of the wife's adulterous activities and actually approved of the activities or forgave the wife. If the wife was conducting extramarital affairs with five other men but the husband knew of only one, the wife could not use condonation as a defense.

3. Connivance. Here the hypothetical becomes slightly more scandalous. Suppose the wife engages in numerous extramarital affairs. The husband is monogamous. The husband files for

divorce, alleging adultery. The husband, however, neglects to mention in the divorce complaint that he was paid for his wife's adulterous affairs. In this case the wife should raise the affirmative defense of "connivance," which is valid when the husband plays an active role in the wife's prostitution. Connivance is presumed to be an affirmative defense for both men and women.

There are two affirmative defenses to inappropriate marital conduct in Tennessee:

1. Insanity. Let's suppose a husband is verbally abusive to his wife. Ever since the wife's second pregnancy the husband refused to be sexually intimate with her or even sleep in the same bedroom with her. The husband is manic depressive, suffers from multiple personality disorder, and had been committed to a state-run mental facility for six months during the course of the marriage. Anxious because of the husband's verbal abuse and worried that it will soon escalate to physical abuse, the wife files for divorce on the grounds of inappropriate marital conduct. The husband should raise an affirmative defense of "insanity." He will have to prove that he did not possess the mental capacity to understand his conduct or to control his actions. Although the insanity defense is not recognized by statute, it is considered valid by Tennessee courts.

2. Justifiable Cause. Suppose the wife stabs the husband repeatedly with a knife. In reaction the husband pushes the wife, and she falls down a flight of stairs. Both parties survive, and the wife files for divorce, claiming the husband's push constituted inappropriate marital conduct. The husband could raise an affirmative defense of "justifiable cause." To use this defense, the husband must be able to prove his wife first tried to stab him and that the push was a reasonable reaction to the wife's provocation.

If a spouse is unable to raise one of these affirmative defenses, the court may find that spouse "at fault" in the divorce. If the parties do not agree to fault in the divorce, raising an affirmative defense could be essential to prevent a spouse from being unfairly found at fault.

Mandatory Injunction

If a party alleges fault grounds (usually inappropriate marital conduct) when a complaint is filed, a temporary injunction can be issued automatically without specific judicial approval. This mandatory injunction (sometimes called "automatic injunction") addresses several topics, including preventing the sale or transfer of certain assets, preventing the dissipation of marital funds, and specifically prohibiting one party from threatening the other with physical harm or harassing the other. The mandatory injunction is effective against both parties at the same time. Make sure you understand the terms of the mandatory injunction if one has been issued in your case. Anyone violating this court order can be jailed for contempt of court. See chapter 1 for the exact terms of the mandatory injunction.

Answer and Countercomplaint

The next step in the legal process is the "answer and countercomplaint." In most divorces the recipient of the complaint for divorce will answer and file a countersuit. The "answer" will most often deny all allegations in the complaint and ask that the complaint be dismissed. The countercomplaint will generally ask for relief similar to that asked for by the plaintiff. The countersuit, called a "countercomplaint," is in essence the same thing as a complaint but against the plaintiff.

How Long Does a Divorce Take?

If there are no children, a mutual-consent, no-fault divorce takes a minimum of sixty days after the filing of the complaint to allow for a "cooling-off" period. If the parties have children, it takes a minimum of ninety days. A contested divorce can last as long as the judge allows it. It could be as few as ninety days or longer than several years. A typical bitterly contested divorce can last from a year and a half to two and a half years. Much of this will depend on the court's docket. If the court is busy, it could take six months or longer to get a trial scheduled.

Annulments and Legal Separation

The court might grant an annulment, that is, a ruling that a legal marriage had never taken place, if the marriage was illegal (i.e., incestuous) or based on fraud or duress. An annulment can also be granted if one party was underage at the time of marriage. The rules and applications can be complex. The law also prevents annulments from causing children to be illegitimate. In an annulment situation alimony is not available, and property rights will be restored as if the marriage had not taken place.

A legal separation (Tennessee calls this a "divorce from bed and board") allows for the court to order support and maintenance of a spouse and divides the marital property without actually granting a final divorce. Either party can sue for an absolute divorce later. The reason most persons should not want a legal separation is that it can be as expensive as a divorce because all the same issues are decided except the divorce itself. The main reason people obtain legal separations is so that one spouse may maintain health insurance through a spouse's employer.

Name Change

Technically, anyone can change his or her name at any time. Generally, it makes sense to do that as part of the divorce process, but it can be done later. The only limitation is that a person cannot change names to perpetrate a fraud or run from creditors. Changing a last name to return to a maiden name is common. If you want to change your name back to your maiden name, tell your lawyer. That will be included in the settlement and/or final decree of divorce.

Courts in Tennessee

Chancellors in Chancery Court and judges in Circuit Court hear divorce matters in Tennessee. In some counties, divorces may be presided over by a General Sessions judge. Once a case is assigned to a particular judge, that case cannot be moved unless the judge recuses himself or herself (declines to hear a case because perhaps the judge knows one or the other spouse), but that is very rare.

When parties cannot settle an issue in a divorce case they go to trial. No attorney can predict with certainty what will happen in any hearing. Once a judge must make a ruling, there is no such thing as a "slam dunk."

In general, a hearing is different from a trial. A trial has specific rules and requires a great deal of planning and preparation. A hearing can be as formal as a trial, but not all the case's issues will be decided. A hearing may take five minutes or several days, just like a trial. Generally, only a trial may be appealed. Many hearings are held on points of law and do not include evidence; it just depends on the issues involved.

In order for a hearing or trial to happen, it has to get on the court's calendar. Some counties hold hearings on regularly scheduled days of the month, and certain counties require special settings for matters that will take longer than two hours. All trials are set specially. Depending on the court's calendar, obtaining that setting could take a week or months.

The process for obtaining a hearing or trial setting can be very challenging. First, the court must have an opening. Next, both lawyers must be available on the date of that opening, and the parties must be able to appear, taking off work if necessary. If there are expert witnesses or key fact witnesses needed, it gets even more difficult. If a lawyer claims to have had improper notice, the judge might agree to reset the hearing. This is called a continuance. Then it might happen that on the day of the reset hearing or trial, the judge, one of the lawyers, or one of the parties is sick, so the case has to be rescheduled again. Well, you get the point. The best way to handle this is to set hearings as fast as possible and do everything possible to avoid delays. But delays can happen even with the best planning.

During contested legal proceedings one or both parties may file motions and petitions. Depending on the court, these terms may mean different things. In motions, a party is asking for a ruling on a point of law, procedure, or fact. Evidence may or may not be considered. For example, a party may file a motion for temporary support. For petitions, an evidentiary hearing may be required.

Discovery

If the parties do not immediately begin settlement negotiations, the next phase of the lawsuit is called "discovery," which most commonly begin with the filing of "interrogatories," which are a set of written questions that must be answered under oath, and a "request for production of documents," which requires the other party to provide certain documents listed in the request. The answers and documents must be produced within thirty days. Other forms of discovery include "depositions," "subpoenas," and "requests for admissions."

The discovery process can be short and inexpensive or lengthy and very expensive. The extent of discovery usually depends on the size and makeup of the marital estate. For example, if one of the parties owns a business that has many employees and produces significant income, the other spouse will most likely hire an expert to review and investigate the books and records of the company to determine its value. Performing a business valuation can be one of the most expensive aspects of any divorce.

In some divorces the attorneys can agree to exchange discovery informally, requesting information and documents without the technical requirements of law, and this can reduce costs significantly. But one reason a lawyer may advise against proceeding with discovery informally even though it saves money is that the answers to questions produced and information supplied by an opposing party will not be under oath. Answering interrogatories under oath means that the person answering the questions is required to tell the complete and full truth and is subject to the criminal penalty of perjury if he or she doesn't. Most divorcing spouses are not willing to commit perjury to gain an advantage in a divorce. Further, if a spouse lies or omits or fails to disclose assets under oath during the discovery process, that lie or omission might be sufficient to undo the divorce based on the fact that the other party relied on misstatements or incomplete production of documents. So requiring the other spouse to provide information and documents formally provides a certain level of protection against fraud.

Depositions are another common form of discovery. An advantage of taking discovery through depositions is that your lawyer will be able to view your spouse live and in action, seeing a performance similar to what might occur in a courtroom if the matter proceeds to trial. Further, with interrogatories and requests for production of documents, there is oftentimes a series of follow-up questions that could be asked concerning the response. In most forms of discovery a lawyer cannot do that, but a deposition will provide that opportunity.

One big disadvantage, however, to the deposition process is that it can be very expensive. During a deposition at least two lawyers will be billing time, and there will be fees for the court reporter's attendance and transcription of the deposition. It is not unusual for a lawyer to spend at least twice the number of hours preparing for a deposition that he or she spends actually taking or defending a deposition. Depositions may take place before or after mediation.

Custody Disputes and Parenting Plans

Divorce creates a new set of parenting challenges for divorcing couples with children. Divorcing parents must be willing to learn that some aspects of their relationship with their children will change, hopefully for the better. In Tennessee, divorcing parents must attend a four-hour parenting-through-divorce class before a divorce is granted. This class emphasizes many important principles that divorcing parents need to learn and apply to their lives, including the important point that it is the parents who are divorcing, not the children.

One of the important aspects of the new parenting plan law is that mediation is mandatory for all divorcing couples before a trial can be held. For more information, see chapter 7, "Mediation and Collaborative Divorce."

There are several methods a court can use to obtain information about the parents and their dispute about which parent should assume the role of primary residential parent. (For a discussion of what is entailed in being a primary residential parent see the discussion in chapter 4, "Custody and Parenting Plans.") One of the most common methods is the appointment of a *guardian ad litem* (GAL). GALs represent children in their best interests. The role of the GAL is dictated by a Supreme Court of Tennessee rule. The GAL will conduct interviews with the children's parents, teachers, neighbors, and day care providers as well as with other persons who are regularly around the children.

Instead of or in addition to a *guardian ad litem*, a court can order an independent child custody evaluation by an experienced and independent court-appointed forensic psychologist. Custody evaluations by psychologists are expensive and will normally be ordered by the court only in cases in which mental illness, drug use, or severe emotional abuse is alleged. The American Psychological Association has issued guidelines for its members who conduct these evaluations, and these can be helpful to read in the event your case involves a custody evaluation. Usually the independent, court-appointed forensic psychologist will conduct psychological testing on both parents and possibly the children, interview the children, and write up a report. The psychologist usually also testifies if there is a trial.

In addition, a party may engage the services of a forensic psychologist as an expert witness. Most often this occurs if one party accuses the other of some form of mental illness. The accused parent can consult with a psychologist so that the psychologist can form and present expert opinion, including possibly refuting the allegations against him or her and defending his or her ability to parent.

If parents agree to a custody arrangement, they must document the agreement in a permanent parenting plan. Tennessee's parenting plan is an approved form issued statewide. The parties can agree to additional terms not included on the form. All parenting plans must be approved by the trial judge. One party must be labeled the primary residential parent. Also, there must be specifics about where the children will stay on school nights, holidays, and summer vacations. In addition, the terms regarding health insurance, life insurance, and other important details are listed. Finally, both parents have certain statutory rights to speak with the children, have access to school records, and see the children at special events such as scouting or athletics. Once it's approved, the parenting plan becomes a court order the court can enforce through its powers to hold a party in contempt.

If the parties cannot agree to a parenting plan, each will file proposed permanent parenting plans with the court before trial, informing the court what they individually believe to be in the best interest of the children. (To learn more about custody and parenting plans, see chapter 4.) Child support worksheets are attached to the permanent parenting plan prior to approval by the court.

Child Support

Determining child support is a very important part of the divorce process. After it's determined who will be the primary residential parent, child support must be agreed upon or set by the court. Pursuant to Tennessee's child support guidelines, the most important factors are the income of both parents and the number of days of parenting time each enjoys. Next, the court considers health insurance costs, child care, and extraordinary expenses. There may be other adjustments and credits to be made depending on the individual circumstances of the case.

The information is plugged into a child support calculator, a program available on the Tennessee Department of Children's Services Web site at http://www.tn.gov/humanserv/is/isdownloads.html. Printouts of the calculations are attached to the permanent parenting plan and become the order of the court. The guidelines are seventy pages long and complicated. (For more detail, please see chapter 5, "Child Support.")

Contempt

When a party violates a part of a court order, the court can enforce the order after the harmed party files a petition for contempt, asking the court to order the violating party to serve time in jail, pay money, or both. There are two types of contempt petitions, civil and criminal. Civil contempt alleges the violation of a court order with which the offending party has the present ability to comply, for instance, paying child support. A court may order that a party found in civil contempt must go to jail until the person complies with the order that was violated. Criminal contempt alleges a past violation of an order and seeks punishment for that violation, which can include jail time. Contempt of court is very serious. Failing to pay court-ordered alimony or child support can result in a jail sentence, having to pay attorney's fees, and a judgment for money owed and interest on that money.

Settlement and Mediation

Most lawyers and judges agree that a settlement will usually be more favorable to both parties than the likely outcome of a contested trial. Settlement is preferred because there are opportunities for compromise and thoroughness in a marital dissolution agreement, the settlement document, that may not arise in a court's ruling. For example, a mother who expects that she will likely be awarded primary residential parent status can negotiate that the father agree to pay certain college expenses for the children. In a divorce trial the trial court has no authority to impose that obligation on the father. Also, divorcing spouses who settle their case often enjoy the privacy that a negotiated settlement can provide as opposed to a trial during which friends and family will likely be called as witnesses, putting the spouses' problems on public display. Finally, voluntary compliance with an agreement is always preferred. Enforcing a trial court's ruling can be very expensive.

Another advantage of the negotiated settlement is that a divorcing party can retain more control. The decision whether to settle a divorce case is the spouse's decision—and *only* the spouse's decision. While a lawyer may recommend in favor of or against a proposed settlement, the final decision still remains in the hands of the client.

The process by which a divorce reaches a negotiated settlement varies from case to case. One common method is that one of the lawyers will be the first to draft and exchange a proposed marital dissolution agreement. If there are children, there is also a proposed permanent parenting plan. The other party can respond by making a counterproposal that requests mediation, seeks discovery, or asks for additional information. Generally, a party will have the right to complete discovery and perform a reasonable investigation into the valuation of the other party's assets prior to being compelled to attend mediation. Mediation is an informal settlement process by which the parties meet with a neutral, third party who has been trained in mediation and sanctioned by the court to deliberate in an informal manner. (Mediation is discussed in more detail in chapter 7.) In divorces, mediation is generally required prior to setting the case for trial.

One bit of good news about mediation is that while many people believe mediation can be a waste of time, money, and effort, statistics show that over 60 percent of cases that are mediated either settle during the mediation process or before trial. In almost all circumstances mediation will save the parties a significant amount of attorneys' fees. Preparing for mediation requires knowing the value of all the other party's assets, knowing the amount of his or her current debts, and having a clear idea of what a reasonable settlement may be.

Depending on the amount of detail learned through discovery, preparing for mediation may require either a little or a great deal of effort. In an average contested case, trial preparation can cost much more than mediation preparation. In the event that settlement negotiations and mediation fail, the case will head toward trial. Some courts will force a trial date on the parties to give them a deadline for negotiations, while other courts will require the parties to apply for a trial date. Preparing for trial can be the most costly of all divorce processes.

Trial Preparation

In preparing for trial, a lawyer must plan for opening statements, direct examination of the client and witnesses, cross-examination of the opposing party and the other party's witnesses, and maybe a closing statement. Other activities include conducting depositions, interviewing witnesses, hiring and preparing expert witnesses for valuations and other expert testimony, organizing the file, choosing and preparing trial exhibits, completing research on legal issues unique to that case, and looking for appellate cases with specific facts and legal issues similar to the case being tried. The lawyer must prepare for each witness to be called, possibly discussing that witness's testimony and determining the best questions to ask. Lawyers also plan to seek to admit documents into evidence and possibly argue to exclude evidence the other party may seek to introduce into evidence. In addition, the lawyer may prepare schedules or other summaries of evidence, charts, and graphs.

Specifically, the court may require preparation and submission of summaries of assets, debts, income, and expenses and summaries of other facts prepared in a very structured format. Depending on the size of the estate, preparing these documents as required by the court can be very time consuming. Making mistakes by omitting assets or income can be very damaging in court. Lawyers must pay particular attention to these details. Clients must be ready to scrutinize their lawyers' work to make sure the listed details are correct.

The client prepares for trial by reading everything the lawyer prepares, assisting with preparing and reviewing documents, and asking questions about the process. Keep in mind that preparing for a trial is a stressful time. In more-complex cases it can take weeks.

In the courtroom the judge will observe all aspects of both spouses' behavior. Be mindful. Dress professionally or as if you were going to church. If you have questions about what clothes to wear, wear the clothes you're considering wearing for court appearances to your lawyer's office so he or she can advise you on whether they are appropriate. Men should always wear a tie and no jewelry other than a watch or one simple ring. Women should wear as little makeup as possible and very little jewelry. Never wear tennis shoes, a T-shirt, shorts, sexually suggestive attire, or any jewelry or pendants that make political or religious statements. The less you say about yourself by your fashion the better. It can distract the judge and can communicate that you do not have the proper respect for the judge and the judicial process. You need to impress the judge that you are taking the trial, the court, and the judge very seriously.

Court appearances make almost everyone nervous, so it's okay to be nervous. Your lawyer can work with you to make you as comfortable as possible. You will not be judged on your performance, on how fast or cleverly you speak. You will be judged on your credibility, so it's critical that you always tell the truth. The most important trial tips will be reserved for your preparation meeting with your lawyer. In that meeting you should learn everything you need to know. If you have questions, that is the time to ask them. (For a more detailed list of testimony tips, see chapter 10.)

Trial

No one wants a trial. They're expensive and unpleasant, and the outcome is never certain. One of the hardest things a lawyer can be called upon to communicate to a client, however, is that trial is sometimes the only alternative to a continuing flood of unreasonable settlement demands or an unwillingness on the part of the opposing side to negotiate at all. Placing your future in the hands of a judge, who is most likely much different from you, is very risky—but it may be necessary.

Court rules require the lawyers to prepare pretrial briefs for the court, outlining the important issues of the case. In a common family law trial, judges will read these briefs before the trial or scan them during opening statements.

The court will decide the following issues at trial:

1. Who will be granted a divorce and on what grounds;
2. What marital and separate property exists, and how the marital assets and debts will be divided;
3. Who will be designated the primary residential parent, and what the allocation of parenting time with the children will be;
4. How much will be awarded in child support;
5. Whether temporary or permanent support in the form of alimony will be awarded;

6. Whether attorney's fees will be awarded; and
7. Against whom court costs will be assessed.

At trial, the plaintiff's lawyer usually speaks first in an opening statement. He or she is followed by the defendant's lawyer's opening statement. The plaintiff's counsel then puts on proof, calling witnesses and introducing documents and items into evidence. After each witness testifies, the defendant's counsel may cross-examine that witness on the testimony just provided. Once the plaintiff's attorney has called all his or her witnesses and sought to introduce all his or her evidence, the plaintiff will rest. Then the defendant's lawyer calls witnesses, seeks to introduce evidence, and then rests as well.

Evidence is introduced in the form of testimony and documents admitted into evidence. An attorney may not testify about the case directly but may testify on issues related to his or her. If needed, a lawyer may issue a subpoena to compel a witness to appear in court or compel others to produce documents, usually financial information. A person who fails to appear or produce documents may be punished by the court.

Either party may be granted a limited opportunity to offer rebuttal testimony. Then the court decides whether to hear closing statements. Some judges skip closing arguments to save time when the evidence and legal issues are clear and no additional legal arguments are needed.

The exact progress and order of a trial is defined by the judge, and only the judge. Both parties have the burden of proving their cases by a preponderance of the evidence. A divorce trial can last from one morning to several weeks. A judge can hear one trial on the issue of custody and then have another trial on the issues of property division and alimony later. Depending on the court's schedule, a judge can receive testimony one day and wait weeks, even months, before continuing again. In other words, it is possible to have a procedure that applies only to your particular case depending on the issues involved, the availability of the court to hear the case, and the availability of witnesses. It's all at the discretion of the court.

Following the attorneys' closing statements, the judge can immediately rule on the case. If the court takes additional time to review the facts and evidence and states an intent to issue a written opinion days or weeks later, this is called taking the matter "under advisement," which is often a very stressful time for the parties. Once the judge rules, the decisions are recorded as a judgment. In divorce cases, the judgment is called the final decree of divorce.

If a divorcing party disagrees with the trial court's ruling, the party may appeal to the Tennessee Court of Appeals. The parties have thirty days following entry of the court's order or ruling on the case to appeal. Normally this is done by filing a "notice of appeal." If either party chooses to appeal the trial court's ruling, he or she is in effect asking the Court of Appeals to find that the trial judge made a mistake.

The time necessary for an appeal usually lasts between nine and eighteen months, depending upon the length of the trial and the complexity and number of legal issues involved. There is no time limit for the Court of Appeals to render its decision. Finally, following the appellate court's decision, either party may ask the Supreme Court of Tennessee to review that decision. That court is not required to hear any particular case. In recent years, the Supreme Court has been hearing about twelve family law cases per year. The Supreme Court's review could take nine to eighteen months.

Most divorcing parties believe that a divorce winds up immediately following a settlement or a ruling by the court, but that's rarely the case. In most divorces there is at least some amount of work to be done after a final decree of divorce is signed by the judge. Examples include but are not limited to preparing, executing, and filing "quit claim deeds" that transfer ownership interests in real property; obtaining refinancing for real property; changing designated beneficiaries on life insurance policies and retirement benefits; drafting, reviewing, executing, and filing "qualified domestic relations orders"; transferring title on automobiles; and transferring possession of property as directed by the court or agreement of the parties. Divorcing parties are often surprised at the expense for completing these transactions.

Learn the process. Ask questions. The more you understand, the more likely you are to get involved and participate in the process. Your lawyer does not know what you know. To get the best results possible you must work together.

Chapter Takeaways:

- Tell the truth, because credibility is vital. If you lose credibility with your judge, you can lose every part of your Tennessee divorce.
- Understand that there is often no such thing as "winning" a divorce. But you can certainly lose a divorce.
- Read, read, read. Learn, learn, learn. The more you read and learn in the beginning of your

Tennessee divorce, the more likely you'll avoid pitfalls.

- Communicate. Keep your legal team informed of important developments. Round up the documents and information your attorney requests in a timely fashion. And ask a ton of questions, because your lawyer can't read your mind. The only stupid question is the one you didn't ask and that your divorce lawyer assumed you had the answer to already.

- Get off Facebook and other social media. Don't assume that none of your "friends" will share with your spouse what you post. As a vindictive response, your spouse may become angrier and refuse to settle even on reasonable terms.

- Team up with your Tennessee divorce lawyer to develop your action plan. Focus time and effort on your important objectives, and then work your plan. When disputes arise over issues that don't impact your major objectives, don't fight over them—save arguing for important matters.

- Take care of yourself. Eat right. Exercise. If you need to get some professional counseling, do so. Don't drink to excess. Get enough sleep. It's okay to say no to others right now, including your friends and parents, and including volunteering at, say, your children's school or church. When you're done with your divorce you can make it up to everyone.

3
Property and Debt Division

Tennessee is an "equitable distribution" state. Equitable distribution means a distribution that is fair, just, and reasonable based on the factors set out in the law. Equitable distribution does not necessarily mean an equal distribution, but most judges will tell you they begin the process by dividing the marital estate 50/50 and then adjust the division one way or the other based on the evidence and arguments presented.

Before property is divided it must be identified, classified, and valued. Identification involves ascertaining all the property owned wholly or in part by the parties. Next, every asset and debt must be classified as either marital or separate. Tennessee courts divide only marital property. Finally, the assets should be valued. While these steps sound simple, like many things in life and divorce, the devil is in the details.

If the spouses are able to agree on how to divide the marital property, then the agreement will be documented in the marital dissolution agreement. Courts in some areas of Tennessee may call it a property settlement agreement. If the parties are unable to agree, the judge will decide and order an equitable distribution of the marital estate at the trial. Every judge would likely divide the property a little differently even if presented with exactly the same assets, debts, and circumstances.

Tennessee Courts consider the following factors when deciding property division:

- The duration of the marriage
- The age, physical and mental health, vocational skills, employability, earning capacity, estate, financial liabilities, and financial needs of each of the parties
- The tangible or intangible contribution by one party to the education, training, or increased earning power of the other party
- The relative ability of each party for future acquisitions of capital assets and income
- The contribution of each party to the acquisition, preservation, appreciation, depreciation, or dissipation of the marital or separate property, including the contribution of a party to the marriage as homemaker, wage earner or parent, with the contribution of a party as homemaker or wage earner to be given the same weight if each party has fulfilled its role

- The value of the separate property of each party
- The estate of each party at the time of the marriage
- The economic circumstances of each party at the time the division of property is to become effective
- The tax consequences to each party, costs associated with the reasonably foreseeable sale of the asset, and other reasonably foreseeable expenses associated with the asset
- The amount of Social Security benefits available to each spouse
- Such other factors as are necessary to consider the equities between the parties

Courts consider the following when deciding how to divide debt:

- The debt's purpose
- Which party incurred the debt
- Which party benefited from incurring the debt
- Which party is best able to repay the debt

As a practical matter, where debt secures a particular asset, a court most often requires the party receiving the asset to pay any and all associated debt and hold the other spouse harmless. The court may also require the party to refinance the debt, removing the other spouse from the liability.

Courts factor in fault only when deciding alimony. As a practical matter, however, if a judge hears evidence of serious fault with respect to a request for alimony or attorney's fees, there is a common belief that the proof can affect property division too as well as other decisions.

Tennessee law defines marital property as follows:

(1)(A) "Marital property" means all real and personal property, both tangible and intangible, acquired by either or both spouses during the course of the marriage up to the date of the final divorce hearing and owned by either or both spouses as of the date of filing of a complaint for divorce, except in the case of fraudulent conveyance in anticipation of filing, and including any property to which a right was acquired up to the date of the final divorce hearing, and valued as of a date as near as reasonably possible to the final divorce hearing date.... . All marital property shall be valued as of a date as near as possible to the date of entry of the order finally dividing the marital property.

(B) "Marital property" includes income from, and any increase in value during the marriage of, property determined to be separate property... if each party substantially contributed to its preservation and appreciation, and the value of vested and unvested pension, vested and unvested stock option rights, retirement or other fringe benefit rights relating to employment that accrued during the period of the marriage.

(C) "Marital property" includes recovery in personal injury, workers' compensation, social security disability actions, and other similar actions for the following: wages lost during the marriage, reimbursement for medical bills incurred and paid with marital property, and property damage to marital property.

(D) As used [here], "substantial contribution" may include, but not be limited to, the direct or indirect contribution of a spouse as homemaker, wage earner, parent or family financial manager, together with such other factors as the court having jurisdiction thereof may determine.

In Tennessee, nonmarital property is the same thing as separate property. Nonmarital property includes the following types of property:

A. All real and personal property owned by a spouse before marriage

B. Property acquired in exchange for property acquired before the marriage

C. Income from and appreciation of property owned by a spouse before marriage except when characterized as marital property under subdivision (b)(1)

D. Property acquired by a spouse at any time by gift, bequest, devise, or descent

E. Pain and suffering awards, victim of crime compensation awards, future medical expenses, and future lost wages

F. Property acquired by a spouse after an order of legal separation where the court has made a final disposition of property.

An inheritance can also be separate property if inherited in the name of the spouse only and if it was segregated (not mixed in) with marital funds. There are ways to prevent an inheritance from becoming marital property and therefore subject to equitable division, but keep in mind that the amount of separate property owned by the spouses is a factor the judge will consider when it comes to dividing the marital property.

Valuation of assets is very important, and depending on the type of asset this can be simple or complicated. Some types of property have a readily ascertainable value, such as a bank account or publicly traded stock. For other assets, if the parties cannot agree on the value, the court will decide. The parties may testify and give an opinion. For some assets, however, the most persuasive proof might be provided by an appraiser or other qualified expert. The most common examples of property that might require professional appraisal and testimony include businesses, pensions, jewelry, and real estate. The valuation process can become expensive especially if both parties hire competing experts.

In Tennessee, assets are to be valued as near the time of the trial as is practical. Tennessee is described as being a "date of distribution" state. This is contrasted with states that require valuations as of the "date of separation." In Tennessee, income earned after the filing of the divorce and appreciation in value of marital property after the filing of the divorce are both marital property subject to division. But as a matter of practice courts often assign debts incurred after the filing of the divorce to the party who incurred the debt. The lessons to be learned here are (1) don't let a divorce linger, allowing your income earned during the divorce to be divided as marital property, and (2) both parties should be frugal because the debt resulting from spending after you file for divorce may be assigned to one party whether that party can afford to pay it or not.

In Tennessee, "dissipation" means wasteful spending. A court must distinguish between those expenditures of marital property that are wasteful and made for the sole benefit of the party making the expenditures and those that may be unwise but are not so much different from the type of expenditures that had been regularly made during the marriage so as to make them destructive.

When determining whether a party has dissipated marital property, a court will generally consider two factors: whether the evidence presented at trial supports the claimed reason for the various expenditures, and, if so, whether that reason equates to dissipation under the circumstances surrounding the expenditures.

The first factor is an objective test. To satisfy this test, the spouse who made the questionable expenditures can offer evidence such as receipts, vouchers, claims, or other similar items that independently support the claimed reason for the expenditures.

The second test entails the court making an equitable determination based upon a number of factors, including:

1. whether a questioned expenditure was the type of expenditure typically made during the marriage
2. who benefited from the questioned expenditure, that is, whether both parties primarily benefited from the expenditure or whether only the spouse making the expenditure primarily benefited
3. how close the expenditure was to the breakdown of the marriage
4. the amount of the expenditure

Examples of dissipation include foolishly spending money, giving money away without benefit to the marital estate, buying jewelry for a paramour, gambling, and spending money for an improper or illegal purpose. Courts do not look favorably upon such activities. Often, courts will determine how much property was dissipated and make a substantial award to the other spouse in an effort counter the effect of the dissipation. This award could be made as part of the property division or ordered to be paid as alimony *in solido*.

The first step in dividing property is to exclude all separate property from the process. Next, the marital estate is divided according to the factors listed above. Then the debt is divided. Debt secured by specific property usually is given to the spouse receiving that property.

Spouses often commingle their marital and nonmarital property. If separate property becomes commingled, it may become marital property. This can cause difficult issues for the court. If separate property can be traced, the court may still divide it as separate property.

Retirement benefits can be considered marital property subject to division by the court to the extent they were acquired during the marriage. Appreciation of marital assets is also divided. These calculations can be very complex. The testimony of a forensic accountant may be required for determining the division of pension assets. Only through expert testimony will the evidence of the value of most defined-benefit plans be admissible at trial. Even though a pension can be legally divided without a valuation, a valuation is highly recommended when a division of pensions affects the overall percentage of property division to the spouses.

The Role of Forensic Accountants and Retirement Assets

When a spouse has a pension through an employer, that person is called the participant, while the other spouse is the non-participant. When representing non-participants, a lawyer must first determine if the pension can be divided in what's called a "separate interest." Some cannot. Many municipal and state pensions are not divisible. If a pension cannot be divided, property division must be considered carefully. A forensic accountant can then ascertain either a reasonable range or a specific present value for benefits due the former employee from the retirement asset. That valuation can then be used to determine an offset against other value in the marital estate. If there are not enough assets in the estate to offset the value of the pension, then the non-participant must negotiate a division of the proceeds when the pension benefits are paid upon retirement. In Tennessee, this is called the "deferred jurisdiction" or "deferred distribution" method. It is complicated and potentially very troublesome to manage. Deferred jurisdiction should always be a last resort.

In general, forensic accountants offer analysis consisting of several steps, assisting in all phases of the litigation. First, the expert may calculate an estimated present value of the pension interest to assist counsel and the client in the very beginning in understanding the scope and the relative importance of the asset in relation to the entire marital estate. Sometimes, even before a complaint is filed, the expert can estimate the present value of the asset for settlement purposes. Later, during the discovery phase, the expert may then interview the client, focus on the details, and prepare a formal report. Then if and when settlement opportunities become exhausted, the formal report can be issued, and preparation for deposition and trial begins. The expert accountant can assist in the review of documents and the opposing party's expert's reports, helping the attorney develop deposition questions. In the post-discovery settlement and pretrial phase, the expert can assist in evaluating final settlement offers. Should the case go to trial, the expert will assist with trial preparations, including exhibits and cross-examination. At trial, the forensic accountant will present a report, testify in support of his report, and refute the opposing party's expert's position.

As retirement benefits have become one of the most important tools employers use to attract valued employees and promote corporate personnel stability, the percentage of divorcing parties' net worth made up of retirement benefits has also increased. In many marital estates, retirement assets account for more than 75 percent of net assets. Division of this category of asset is often misunderstood. A mistaken valuation can cause a devastating, one-sided financial result. Pension valuations are serious business.

Each retirement plan is unique, so there are different valuation techniques. Pension valuation is not an exact science. Statistics, actuarial tables, government reports, tax tables, investment market knowledge, and professional judgment all play important roles in the process.

Most but not all pensions are divisible. A divorce attorney may rely on a forensic accountant to review the pension document to confirm that a given retirement asset is divisible. After a trial or settlement, if a pension is divisible, pensions are divided by means of a document known as a "qualified domestic relations order" (QDRO). The QDRO will be drafted by either lawyer or an attorney specializing in pensions engaged by one or both lawyers and can be entered as an order of the court within thirty to ninety days following entry of the final decree of divorce.

Identifying, classifying, and valuing marital property and determining the facts needed for debt division are just the beginning. Each type of asset requires knowing specific information. For example, there are many different types of life insurance policies: some have cash surrender values, while others have annuities as a separate investment component. For life insurance policies, spouses need the policies, declaration pages, recent benefits statements or summaries, and supporting schedules if applicable. Getting the needed information and documents as early in the case as possible is very important.

Intellectual Property Rights

Royalties and other streams of cash are paid on patents, trademarks, copyrights, trade secrets, and other types of "intellectual" property. They can be very valuable, and valuing them depends primarily upon one thing—expected future cash flow. There are experts who can value these assets for divorce purposes. Whether the intellectual property is a song or a complex chemical patent, never ignore such assets even if the other spouse tells you, "Oh, it's not worth a dime."

Business Valuation in Tennessee Divorce

The valuation of a publicly traded corporation is relatively simple, but in the case of a business owned by a spouse, its valuation can be extremely complex. An expert will likely be required to offer evidence of its value. The exact process depends on the type of business. For professional practices, specific valuation techniques are used, and personal goodwill is generally not considered.

You have to take great care when it comes to valuing a business, particularly when it's the most substantial asset in a divorce. Opposing business valuation experts may value the same closely held business quite differently. The difference can result in two valuations literally millions of dollars apart. The attorney must have a depth of understanding with regards to valuation methods, accounting, and finance. All methods used to value a business are filled with subjective value judgments. The attorney must be able to understand the subtle but common errors that can occur with each valuation method to prevent prejudice to his or her client's case. Complicated valuation issues are especially challenging to argue in front of a judge who may have no education, training, or experience whatsoever in economics, finance, or business-appraisal theory.

Getting the right business valuation expert for your case is critical. Your family law attorney may have worked with many of the area's most experienced valuation experts, also called business appraisers. All business valuation experts have credentials issued from the leading national organizations such as the American Institute of CPAs (AICPA), the American Society of Appraisers (ASA), the National Association of Certified Valuation Analysts (NACVA), and the Institute of Business Appraisers (IBA). In making your decision, you must consider each prospective expert's experience, reputation, cost, and ability to explain extremely complex economic and valuation theories in terms simple enough for your judge to understand.

In many circumstances the debt of a business can become more important than the intrinsic value of the business. If one spouse owns a business and has pledged personal (i.e., marital) assets as security for debt, the other spouse should be careful to determine the total amount of debt and protect himself or herself against being held liable for those debts. These important issues must be addressed in the marital dissolution agreement.

Professional Practices in Divorce

In Tennessee, a professional license or degree of a doctor, dentist, CPA, lawyer, or other professionals is generally not considered an asset subject to valuation and division. While the license or degree itself cannot be divided, the professional practice or certain of its assets could be subject to valuation and division in certain circumstances. This is a very complicated and often misunderstood area of law. Valuation of and division of professional practices are discussed in detail in chapter 11.

Chapter Takeaways:

- Identify all assets. How can you divide a marital estate if you don't know it exists or what's in it? If you think your spouse is hiding assets, talk with your lawyer and consider hiring a forensic accountant.
- Classify all assets as marital or separate property under Tennessee law. If the issues are complicated, consider hiring a forensic accountant to help.
- Value all assets and debts. Pay particular attention to businesses, professional practices, pensions, stock options, and intellectual property such as copyrights and patents. If there is a business to value, consider hiring a business valuation expert, also called a business appraiser.
- Read and study the factors for property division. Share with your lawyer every important fact and piece of evidence, good and bad, applicable to the factors.
- Determine a reasonable expectation of what percentage of marital property you should end up with.

- Focus all negotiations with your desired percentage of marital property in mind.

To learn more about property division, business valuations, and asset investigations, see www.MemphisDivorce.com. For a much more detailed discussion, see *The Forensic Accounting Deskbook: A Practical Guide to Financial Investigation and Analysis for Family Lawyers,* by Miles Mason, Sr. JD, CPA. In particular, see chapter 7, "Asset Identification, Classification, and Valuation—From Simple to Complex." For ordering information go to www.ForensicAccountingDeskbook.com.

4

Custody and Parenting Plans

A permanent parenting plan (PPP) is a detailed, written outline providing for parenting in the best interests of the children. Many states, including Tennessee, offer these on standardized forms. PPPs allow both spouses to divide up parenting responsibilities, establish a residential schedule, and set child support. A residential schedule outlines when the children are in each parent's physical care and designates the primary residential parent. The residential schedule also states the details concerning in which parent's home the children shall reside on given days of the year, including holidays, birthdays, vacations, and other special occasions. Time with children is "parenting time" or "residential time" and is no longer legally referred to as "visitation," although that term is still in common use. If you have children and want a divorce, you will be required to agree upon a PPP and attend a four-hour parenting class (see www. MemphisDivorce.com for a class list in Memphis).

If you and the other parent are able to agree on a permanent parenting plan that is approved by the approved by the court, the PPP becomes an order that the court may enforce with its contempt powers. If you and your spouse cannot agree on a PPP, you must first go to mediation and try to agree on one before the court will try your case.

Technically, "primary residential parent" means the parent with whom the children resides more than 50 percent of the time. In most cases, however, the primary residential parent will have the children on school nights and school mornings. In general, parents share equally weekends, holidays, and special events.

Permanent parenting plan forms read: "Each parent will make decisions regarding the day-to-day care and control of each child while the child is residing with that parent." Most parenting decisions fall under the "day-to-day" designation. The "custodial parent" and "primary residential parent" designations are not exactly the same. Under prior law, custodial parent generally meant the parent who exercised final decision-making authority and the parent with whom the children primarily resided. Under Tennessee's parenting plan law, these concepts are split. Final decision-making authority is discussed separately from residential time and can be fragmented between the parents by category, including education, extracurricular activities, nonemergency health care, and religious training.

Reaching an agreement on a permanent parenting plan can be challenging. If no agreement is reached, mediation is required. For those parents seeking divorce who get along, this should not pose a serious problem. Parents who cannot agree and do not get along will have to invest a serious amount of time and resources. In theory this investment should pay dividends in the long run, reducing the need and expense of returning to the court system when parenting conflicts arise.

Proposed PPPs must be filed and served no less than forty-five days before the trial date. If one parent fails to file a proposed PPP, he or she runs the risk of having the other parent's plan approved by default. Each proposed PPP must include an attached statement of income and expenses and be signed under oath that the plan was proposed in good faith and in the best interest of the children.

Strategically, parents who are not represented by an attorney can be at a serious disadvantage in this matter. Relying on the statements of an opposing spouse who is represented can be damaging, especially if the statements are not completely candid. As before the new law, the first few decisions following separation or filing the divorce are critical. Under the new parenting plan law, waiting to take action can seriously damage a case.

Without a doubt, the new parenting law can create opportunities for parents to put aside differences and address the actual best interests of the children. While the new law creates an additional layer of bureaucracy for every divorcing parent, it will be just the uninformed parent who gets hurt by this.

Custody Determination

Every PPP must name the primary residential parent and include a parenting time schedule. If these are not agreed upon, the court will make sure there are residential provisions for each child consistent with the child's developmental level and the family's social and economic circumstances. Courts try to encourage both parents to maintain a loving, stable, and nurturing relationship with their children. In figuring out which parent should serve as the primary residential parent, Tennessee courts will consider the following factors:

(a) In a suit for annulment, divorce, separate maintenance, or in any other proceeding requiring the court to make a custody determination regarding a minor child, the determination shall be made on the basis of the best interest of the child. In taking into account the child's best interest, the court shall order a custody arrangement that permits both parents to enjoy the maximum participation possible in the life of the child consistent with the factors set out in subdivisions (a)(1)-(10), the location of the residences of the parents, the child's need for stability and all other relevant factors. The court shall consider all relevant factors, including the following, where applicable:

(1) The love, affection and emotional ties existing between the parents or caregivers and the child;

(2) The disposition of the parents or caregivers to provide the child with food, clothing, medical care, education and other necessary care and the degree to which a parent or caregiver has been the primary caregiver;

(3) The importance of continuity in the child's life and the length of time the child has lived in a stable, satisfactory environment; provided, that, where there is a finding, under subdivision (a) (8), of child abuse, as defined in § 39-15-401 or § 39-15-402, or child sexual abuse, as defined in § 37-1-602, by one (1) parent, and that a nonperpetrating parent or caregiver has relocated in order to flee the perpetrating parent, that the relocation shall not weigh against an award of custody;

(4) The stability of the family unit of the parents or caregivers;

(5) The mental and physical health of the parents or caregivers;

(6) The home, school and community record of the child;

(7) (A) The reasonable preference of the child, if twelve (12) years of age or older;

(B) The court may hear the preference of a younger child on request. The preferences of older children should normally be given greater weight than those of younger children;

(8) Evidence of physical or emotional abuse to the child, to the other parent or to any other person; provided, that, where there are allegations that one

(1) parent has committed child abuse, as defined in § 39-15-401 or § 39-15-402, or child sexual abuse, as defined in § 37-1-602, against a family member, the court shall consider all evidence relevant to the physical and emotional safety of the child, and determine, by a clear preponderance of the evidence, whether such abuse has occurred. The court shall include in its decision a written finding of all evidence, and all findings of facts connected to the evidence. In addition, the court shall, where appropriate, refer any issues of abuse to the juvenile court for further proceedings;

(9) The character and behavior of any other person who resides in or frequents the home of a parent or caregiver and the person's interactions with the child; and

(10) Each parent's or caregiver's past and potential for future performance of parenting responsibilities, including the willingness and ability of each of the parents and caregivers to facilitate and encourage a close and continuing parent-child relationship between the child and both of the child's parents, consistent with the best interest of the child.

No one factor controls; each factor must be weighed and considered in relation to the others. Note that any of the above factors may be overshadowed by:

- abandonment
- substantial refusal to perform parenting responsibilities
- physical or sexual abuse of a child or parent
- emotional or physical impairment interfering with parenting responsibilities
- drug, alcohol, or other substance abuse
- abusive use of conflict that endangers the children's psychological development
- withholding the other parent's access to the children without good cause
- a parent's criminal conviction
- any other factors adverse to children

Obviously, these important considerations can weigh most heavily if they can be proven.

If there is a trial, mothers are not always more likely to be granted primary residential parent status. The parenting plan law states: "It is the legislative intent that the gender of the party seeking to be the primary residential parent shall not give rise to a presumption of parental fitness or cause presumption in favor of or against such party." All things being equal, a mother is still more likely to be granted primary residential parent status and to be awarded final decision-making authority, but not for the reasons one might expect. One reason may be that the mother may have more time to devote to the children than a father employed in a demanding profession. Another reason may be that the mother may have more experience and may have established a successful track record in raising the parties' children.

In certain situations, as was the case for a couple from Germantown, Tennessee, the father had fulfilled the traditional primary caregiving role prior to the divorce and received full custody after a trial. A father with an established parenting track record is as likely to be awarded primary residential parent status for the same reason a mother may have in the past. In most cases it is the caregiving role performed prior to the divorce and/or during the divorce, not the party's gender, that creates this advantage or disadvantage.

As children get older, fathers' opportunities increase to be designated primary residential parents, especially with teenage boys, due to a perceived greater need for "male nurturing" and lesser need for traditional "caregiving." The time a parent has available and his or her track record with the children are very important factors. Discrimination based on gender is prohibited by the Tennessee and U. S. Constitutions.

According to Tennessee law, if the children are over twelve, the court will hear and consider their preferences for a parent. If children are under twelve, courts rarely choose to hear and consider the children's wishes. The older the children, the stronger those wishes may be considered. Understand that courts do not look favorably on children being coerced or coached. Involving children in the aspects of a difficult divorce, such as urging them to choose between parents, could cause them to end up with long-lasting feelings of guilt, which might seriously harm them.

Status quo matters. If children are healthy, happy, and well-adjusted, courts are reluctant to make a change. Courts are less likely to disrupt an acceptable situation in favor of the unknown. All things being equal, maintaining stability can be a judge's most important concern.

Courts want to keep siblings together. There must be a compelling, reasonable, and practical reason for splitting up siblings. Even if the divorcing parents agree to split siblings, a court may reject the proposed arrangement.

If a parent has a live-in companion or other person sharing the home with children, that situation can also impact a court's decision of who will be designated as primary residential parent. Before a divorce is granted, most courts severely frown upon children being exposed to their parents' new romantic relationships. In situations where another person will come in contact with or influence the children by reason of a remarriage or similar changes in the children's or parent's living situation and there is a basis for concern about the stability of the children's environment, the mental condition and character of that other person can become the central focus in a custody dispute.

The relative wealth of a parent is only one factor that goes into determining who will be chosen by the court as primary residential parent, but a wealthy parent may be considered better able to offer educational opportunities. As anyone would expect, however, the more-devoted parent who sacrificed and made time for children will almost always prevail over a wealthy parent. In these cases, priorities often become the central issue.

In Tennessee, "shared parenting" can mean more than one thing. Shared parenting means children will spend exactly or roughly equal time with both parents. Under prior law in Tennessee, the term "joint custody" had more than one meaning. In a true joint custody situation, parents share the final decision-making authority. For other cases, one parent had been labeled the primary custodial parent, and that parent had final decision-making authority, and in most situations the children would have resided with that parent. Visitation was a separate issue from custody. Some of these labeling problems are solved by Tennessee's current parenting plan law. For example, if parents are to share final decision-making authority and there is a dispute, the method for resolution of that dispute must be spelled out. Most likely the courts will require mediation prior to setting a hearing to resolve a dispute. By splitting the designation of parenting or residential time from decision-making authority and by eliminating the words "custody" and "visitation" from the new vocabulary, the parenting plan law hopes to seriously reduce custody wars and encourage co-parenting.

Even where there is shared parenting, one parent will owe the other parent child support. The parent with whom the children reside more often will receive child support from the non-primary residential parent.

Allegations of abuse are relevant and important but technically not controlling. Where abuse is shown to have affected the children, the court will consider this along with the other factors discussed above. Courts look at abuse allegations closely for obvious reasons. If a court believes a spouse has made a false accusation of abuse to gain advantage in litigation, the consequences will be serious.

PPP Operations

Each parent has final decision-making authority over decisions regarding the day-to-day care and control of the children while the children are residing with that parent. In any event, however, a parent's authority is never really absolute. An aggrieved parent disagreeing with the parent with final decision-making authority can initiate mediation to "discuss" the other parent's decision on the grounds that the challenged action is not in the best interest of the children. This request for mediation, under the requirements of the parenting plan, could be the first step to challenging the decision in court and ultimately can end up being the basis for a claim that the designation of primary residential parent be changed. Judges, though, will rarely overrule a parent's decision unless the decision endangers children or affects the children's best interests in a meaningful way.

Tennessee has set out the rights of a parent during those times when the children are not in the care of that parent. That parent has the right:

- To unimpeded telephone conversations with the children at least twice each week at reasonable times and for a reasonable duration
- To send mail to the children that the other parent shall not open and will not censor
- To receive notice and relevant information as soon as practical (but within twenty-four hours) in the event of hospitalization, major illness, or death of the child
- To receive directly from the school copies of the children's report cards, attendance records, names of teachers, class schedules, standardized test scores, and any other records customarily made available to parents
- Unless otherwise provided by law, to receive copies of the children's medical, health, or other

treatment records directly from the physician or health care provider who provided such treatment or health care

- To be free of derogatory remarks made about such parent or such parent's family by the other parent to or in the presence of the children
- To be given at least forty-eight hours' notice, whenever possible, of all extracurricular activities, and the opportunity to participate or observe in those activities, including but not limited to school, church, and athletic activities and other activities during which parental participation or observation would be appropriate
- To receive from the other parent, in the event the other parent leaves the state with the minor children for more than two days, an itinerary, including telephone numbers, for use in the event of an emergency
- To access and participate in the children's education, including the right of access to the minor children for lunch and other activities, on the same basis that is provided to all parents

If a parent fails to pay child support, parenting time will be terminated only in the rarest of circumstances. Ways of collecting child support include filing a petition for contempt seeking to put the nonpaying parent in jail. On the other hand, if the primary residential parent refuses the other parenting time for any reason, there is recourse. Proper enforcement of visitation or parenting time rights begins with filing a petition or referring the matter to mediation. Persistent violation of a court-ordered right to visitation or parenting time can be grounds for a change of primary residential parent.

There are only a few things in life more difficult or more expensive than disputes over parenting time and final decision-making authority. Be sure that you want these designations for the right reasons. Examples of wrong reasons include the need for child support, unwillingness to pay child support, fear of societal judgment, and anger. You will need to be able to prove the children will live a better life with you. This means evidence of this, so plan ahead.

There are many good books and parenting magazines available. Read them. There is no substitute for informed decision-making and sound judgment. Discuss your situation thoroughly with your experienced family law attorney and with those you trust to give you sound advice.

Parenting Time

"Parenting time" means the same as "residential time." Both terms replace "visitation," but visitation described only the time the non-custodial parent enjoyed with the children. Now, both parents have parenting time or residential time.

Why do separated parents fight so often over visitation? The fights aren't always really about visitation. Often, one parent is looking for an opportunity to spite the other or exert some type of control. Separated parents who are able to work together may be able to avoid all kinds of pain and suffering compared to separated parents who do not cooperate. Disputes over parenting time can be the most emotionally taxing fights any former couple may have. Tension builds, and tempers flare.

All of a sudden the former couple is back into their routine they both believed they'd left behind, and the children are the victims.

What can judges do to reduce conflict? Because judges have heard so many frivolous visitation arguments they have moved toward requiring much-more detailed parenting arrangements. Tennessee's parenting plan law also requires most arguing parents to head to mediation before bringing a dispute to court. Working out the details of parenting in advance costs less in the long run financially and emotionally. Few things in life are more painful than filing a petition with the court two years after a divorce to rework a poorly planned PPP.

A parent living far from the children presents unique problems. Normal visitation schedules are impossible, and transportation costs become very important. How many weeks of visitation will there be in the summer? During Christmas? Spring break? How many visits will be allowed if the parent travels to the children? Are travel days counted in the number of days allowed? Almost every possible parenting time arrangement will require both parents to compromise.

Outside of regularly scheduled visitation, when may a primary residential parent deny visitation? A visitation request should not be denied unless the request is unreasonable. Common sense should help guide both parents. Visitation should not last late into the evening on a school night. Visitation should not require children to regularly wake up extremely early, cause them to miss important school or extracurricular activities, or otherwise interfere with a normal upbringing.

If the matter goes to litigation, limitations on visitation may depend on your judge's values. Like most things in family law, what is "reasonable" parenting time depends on the facts and circumstances of each situation.

Some advice to the future primary residential parent: be flexible with visitation. From the perspective of the children, the absent parent can become the perfect parent. Understand that if the other parent is a complete loser, the children will learn this soon enough for themselves. Even if the other parent is obnoxious and does not appreciate your efforts, work as hard as you can for the children's sake. Also, remember that you do not want to go to court to argue about residential-time issues. Rarely do the dollars spent litigating pay off in the long run except to prove a point. Also, think of the other parent's residential time as free babysitting. Take advantage of the time alone. Go on a date. Have fun. Read a book. Enjoy some quiet time. Finally, a parent who regularly spends time with the children is more likely to pay child support on time.

If the parents routinely share parenting time flexibly and without regard to the parenting plan, that will cause a problem only if there is a dispute in the future about parenting time or child support. Deviating from the PPP a few nights a year here and there should not cause concern because that is natural and preferable, but dramatically changing the parenting time in day-to-day living can create a legal problem. Keep in mind that child support is based on the number of nights the children spend with each parent. After entry of the PPP, the other parent may be spending more time with the children with the intention of getting a modification of parenting time based on actual nights.

If the PPP is modified, it could set up an argument that the other parent should pay less child support based on the increased number of nights he or she has the children. If you have concerns along those lines, speak to your family lawyer and get advice about your specific situation before you make decisions you may regret.

Parenting Disputes

In general, what's in the best interests of the children is the guiding principle when dealing with contested issues involving children in divorce. Just as parents do, judges differ on how they believe children should be raised. Never assume the judges will see things as you see them. Judges and lawyers likely have different parenting values. While the parents' values are more important, it is not unusual for value differences to impact rulings and settlements.

In most disputed custody cases, courts will award most school nights and school mornings to the parent with a track record of success as the primary caregiver and the parent who will more likely foster and encourage a relationship between the children and the other parent. If the judge perceives one parent acting as the emotionally aggrieved victim or acts out like an angry parent seeking to use the children as tools for revenge, the judge will be less likely to designate that parent primary residential parent.

When facing a parenting dispute, make sure you follow the basic, unwritten rules. When in doubt about what to tell your children about the divorce, assure them that both parents love them. Make every effort to spend time with your children during this difficult period. Learn everything possible about handling the tough questions that will come. Never give children messages to deliver to the other parent. Avoid asking children what visitation they want with the other parent, because making them choose between parents is unfair. Only parents should determine visitation. And do everything possible not to interrogate the children for intelligence-gathering purposes after visits with the other parent. If you are concerned your children are hurting, seek family counseling with a competent and experienced mental health professional.

Intentional alienation of children's affection toward the other parent is a charge no one ever wants to defend in court. Never argue in front of the children—judges don't care what the argument was about. Never call the other parent the words that come to mind if children can hear, even if the words are true. Derogatory comments are forbidden by the mandatory injunction. In addition, be vigilant in stopping your friends and family members from talking badly of the other parent in front of the children. And never listen in to conversations with the other parent unless you legitimately fear there is some sort of abuse.

Children need to know both parents love them and little about the divorce itself. Parents should avoid discussing with the children details of the divorce even if the details are true. Telling children "the truth" about what is going on should never be used as an excuse to discuss the divorce. Plus telling children, regardless of their ages, that the other parent is a dirtbag tends to create sympathy for the other parent. As well, the absent parent can become an idealized, perfect parent. Always encourage parenting time with the other parent. Never restrict parenting time just to punish the other parent.

Children want to love both their parents. Some children may want their parents to reconcile. Some may even develop unhealthy and unrealistic expectations of what might happen.

Some children may blame themselves for the breakup. If you see your children acting out or have other behavioral problems, talk to the other parent and seek professional help together.

You should also read as much about co-parenting as possible; you'll find many books and articles on the topic. Learn the terms and language used. Understand that the primary residential parent should be the parent who is more likely to meet the other parent more than halfway.

Equal Time

Some parents may want to share roughly equal time or share parenting equally. This is controversial. Some judges have very specific ideas about whether this is a good idea. Whether equal time involves rotating weeks or some other creative logistical solution, for this type of parenting schedule to work, both parents must be committed to communicating, sharing, and working together. If not, the equal time solution may do more harm than good.

Some mothers see time away from parenting as an opportunity to focus on their careers, work late on school nights, work out, or date. On the other hand, some fathers may learn that single parenting is not as glamorous as it seems. The daily grind of homework, transporting children to extracurricular activities, and household maintenance can be taxing for a couple let alone a single parent. The key here is the commitment to true co-parenting. If either parent is looking to escape the reality that parenting is hard or is seeking to pay less in child support, equal-time parenting will not work well, and the children will suffer for it.

Custody Battle 101

If you find yourself in a bitter custody contest, what should you do? Talk over strategies with your lawyer. Will mediation work? Will your spouse agree to attend post-separation family counseling? Is there a compromise you both can live with? A custody battle is one of the most destructive types of litigation. But sometimes custody litigation cannot be avoided.

Many judges feel that children's best interests are served by spending the majority of school nights and school mornings in one household with one parent. And as a matter of physics, children cannot spend the night in two places at one time. One parent may need to have a vast majority of school nights and school mornings for consistency. Without that consistency, children may become confused and disoriented by two different environments and parenting styles relating to homework, studying, and school projects.

To "win" a custody battle requires doing everything possible to be the most perfect parent possible. Avoid stupid mistakes. Avoid drinking and drugs. Never argue in front of the children. Don't spend the night away from your children. Know each of your children's teachers and communicate with them about your children. Help your children with their homework. Talk to your children's counselors. Follow all the unwritten rules discussed.

Include your spouse in parenting decision-making even if it kills you. Being right is not always the most important goal. Demonstrating a willingness to cooperate with the other parent may be a more effective strategy than making better decisions on your own. Many judges notice and appreciate this. Be the bigger parent. Study the custody factors. Discuss your parenting strengths and weaknesses with your lawyer. If you don't know them, learn them. Try to fix your parenting weaknesses.

If there ever was a time for you to be the adult and focus every part of your life on parenting, this is it. Judges expect parents in a custody battle to be on their best behavior. Judges will look sternly on any decision making that demonstrates that the children are not that parent's highest priority. Surreptitiously recording the other parent in conversation will likely backfire. It sends a message that the recording parent likely cannot manage the relationship in the best interest of the children. Plus, recording the other parent is viewed as a dirty tactic.

There are many, many books on child custody battle tactics and strategies. Many of the custody battle books are filled with legal advice that is either bad advice or advice that won't apply to you and your situation. Some are downright destructive in tone. If you want to read more about custody battles, ask your lawyer. But your first and most important obligation is to develop a strategy with your lawyer and stick to it. Changing direction in the middle of you case can send mixed signals to your spouse and the court, and this can damage your case and make settlement more difficult than it needs to be.

The Greatest Non-Primary
Residential Parent Ever

If you find yourself likely to be the non-primary residential parent (or in child support terms, the ARP, the alternative residential parent), you should take solace in the idea of working hard to be the best non-primary residential parent ever. This is easy to do and is much less expensive in terms of legal fees. Always be available to help your children with homework. Don't be a "Disney World Dad," one who's there only to have fun with the children. Support the primary residential parent in education, discipline, religious upbringing, and financially so your children may have the extras in the future you want them to have.

Try to negotiate that you should have the right of first refusal to watch the children if the primary residential parent must be away from the children even just for a few hours. Try to negotiate evenings during the week. If you have the children on school evenings, focus on knowing all their homework assignments and help them get those completed. Volunteer to help with school projects or math homework if you are better at math. Negotiate for as much time as you can logistically manage in the summers. And be willing to trade off time when scheduling trips on fall breaks, spring breaks, and summer vacations. What goes around generally comes around.

Flexibility is the goal, not absolute control. For example, if the children are scheduled to be with you on a particular evening and the other parent gets Grizzlies (Memphis's NBA team) tickets at the last minute and wants to take the kids, let the other parent do so. There may be a time you get offered free tickets to some event at the last minute. If you and the other parent share this sort of flexibility, you both "win."

Relocation Law

Tennessee's "Parent Relocation Statute" sets out the course of action for divorced parents when one parent wishes to relocate the children outside the state or more than 100 miles from the other parent within the state. The relocating parent is required to send written notice to the nonrelocating parent no later than sixty days prior to the move. The nonrelocating parent then has thirty days after receiving the notice to object to the court. If the nonrelocating parent does not object within thirty days, he or she may not be able to object later.

The statute differentiates between parents who spend substantially equal amounts of time with the children and those who do not. The statute does not require for the time spent with the children to be exactly equal between the parents, only for it to be substantially equal. The Tennessee Court of Appeals, in *Monroe v. Robinson,* held that the parents spent substantially equal amounts of time with the children when the father had the children for approximately 43 percent of the time and the mother had the children for approximately 57 percent of the time. The court, however, concluded in *Connell v. Connell* that the parents did not spend substantially equal amount of time with the children when the father had the children for approximately 40 percent of the time. These decisions demonstrate the individuality of the circumstances in each case. Because neither the statute nor Tennessee case law specifically set out what constitutes substantially equal amounts of time, the court must examine the particularities of each case.

If the court finds that the parents spend substantially equal amounts of time with the children, no presumption in favor or against the request for relocation shall arise. Instead, the court determines whether to permit relocation of the children based upon the children's best interests. The statute sets out a list of factors that can be used to determine whether the relocation would be in the children's best interest. Some of these factors are:

- the extent to which visitation rights have been allowed and exercised
- whether the primary residential parent, once out of the jurisdiction, is likely to comply with any new visitation arrangement
- the love, affection, and emotional ties between the parents and children
- the stability of the family unit of the parents

The statute, however, designates a different procedure for parents who do not spend substantially equal amounts of time with their children. If the parent proposing the relocation spends the greater amount of time with the children, the relocation will not be prevented unless it does not have a reasonable purpose, it would pose a threat of serious or specific harm to the children, or the relocating parent's motive for relocating is vindictive, perhaps to make it hard for the nonrelocating parent to visit the children.

The nonrelocating parent has the burden of proving that one of these three factors exists. If one of the three listed factors is present, the court will determine whether the relocation is in the children's best interests by consulting the factors in the previous paragraph.

The intent behind the parent relocation statute is to prevent one parent from packing up and moving the children without the consent of the nonrelocating parent and the court. The statute aims to keep the children's best interest as the most important priority when determining whether relocation is appropriate. The relocation of one of the parents may affect child support and may lead the court to assess the costs of transporting the children for visitation.

If you think you or your spouse is likely to move after the divorce, immediately discuss this with your lawyer. Those issues are very important and should be incorporated into your preparation of a parenting plan.

Grandparent Visitation

The Tennessee legislature has enacted laws that enable grandparents to seek visitation rights with their grandchildren in particular situations. In most divorces, grandparents visit when the parents set it up. These laws were enacted when parents refused to allow such visitation. In these cases, one or more grandparents sue the parent or parents denying visitation. These cases are usually expensive and difficult. If you anticipate grandparent-visitation issues, discuss the situation with your lawyer and do everything possible to work out these issues out of court.

Chapter Takeaways:

- Read and study the factors for Tennessee custody. Share with your lawyer every important fact and piece of evidence, good and bad, applicable to the factors.
- If you have been the primary caregiver for the children, be prepared to prove it.

- If the children are happy, healthy, well-adjusted, and have good grades, and you were their primary caregiver, be prepared to prove it.
- If the other parent has engaged in an inappropriate activity, be prepared to prove it. Talk to your lawyer about possibly hiring a private investigator.
- If you have concerns over the other parent's mental health, be prepared to substantiate them. Consider asking the court to appoint a forensic psychologist to perform an independent child custody evaluation or court-ordered mental evaluation.
- Understand that there is often no such thing as "winning" a custody battle. Keep your children out of disputes. Even if you are honest and heartfelt in discussing your divorce with your children, the judge will likely hold this against you.
- Don't date. Focus your efforts on demonstrating to the court that your children are your first priority.

5
Child Support

Tennessee's child support guidelines are rules put out by the Tennessee Department of Human Services, Child Support Division and modified every few years. So always check to make sure you have the current set of guidelines.

In 2005, the rules dramatically changed to the Income Shares Model, taking into account the income of both parents, the number of overnights enjoyed by each parent, and other key expenses such as health insurance and child care. The guidelines are lengthy, detailed, and complex, so the discussion here is a general overview. Know that exceptions may apply to any situation. To get the answer to a specific question, consult with an experienced family law attorney.

Interpretations of the guidelines will be determined by the Tennessee Court of Appeals and the Supreme Court of

Tennessee. But because some of the guidelines' provisions are relatively new, some important interpretations may not come out for years to come.

The parent who pays child support is the alternative residential parent (ARP), and the parent who receives child support is the primary residential parent, (PRP). The child support worksheets are forms and a calculator used to input a lot of information to determine the amount of support. Links to the guidelines and the calculator are at www.MemphisDivorce.com on its "Child Support" pages.

Basic Child Support Obligation

Determining child support begins with determining the basic child support obligation (BCSO), the expenses child support is designed to cover. Expenses include an average amount to cover child-rearing expenses that include housing, food, and transportation. The share of total expenditures devoted to clothing and entertainment is also included in the BCSO, but it's relatively small compared to the other three items. Basic educational expenses based on a public school education (such as fees, books, and local field trips) is also included in the BCSO.

The BCSO does not include health insurance premiums for the children, work-related childcare costs, a child's uninsured medical expenses, special expenses, or extraordinary educational expenses because of how much these can vary among different families.

The first step to calculate the BCSO is to obtain the gross income of each parent. Gross income includes all income from any source (before taxes and other deductions), whether earned or unearned, and includes:

- wages
- salaries
- commissions
- fees
- tips
- income from self-employment
- fringe benefits
- bonuses
- severance pay
- pensions or retirement plans (including Social Security)
- Veteran's Administration
- Railroad Retirement Board, Keoghs
- individual retirement accounts
- interest, dividend, and trust income
- annuities
- capital gains
- disability or retirement benefits received from Social Security (whether paid to the parent or to the child based on the parent's account)
- workers compensation (temporary or permanent)
- unemployment insurance benefits
- judgments to recover for personal injuries and awards from other civil actions
- gifts of cash or things that can be converted to cash
- prizes and lottery winnings

• alimony or maintenance received from other persons other than parties to the proceeding before the tribunal

As you can see, gross income is a very broad category. The wealth of a stepparent or other person residing with a child is not considered in setting child support awards.

The second step is to calculate the adjusted gross income (AGI) of each parent by subtracting "credits" from the gross income of each parent. Credits allow a parent to reduce the amount of gross income that is used to calculate the BCSO. These credits are:

• self-employment tax
• a child supported in the parent's home
• a child supported by the parent under a child support case
• a child who does not live in the parent's home and is receiving support from the other parent but not pursuant to a court order

Credits are available for both children under preexisting and subsequent orders. For credit purposes, preexisting orders are directly deducted from the gross income of a parent. A parent is given the full amount of credit. No credit is given for overdue payments. To receive credit for children who are under a support order, a parent must prove they are actually providing support for those children. To receive credit for children not under a support order, the parent claiming the credit must prove that he or she has a legal obligation to support the child and are actually doing so.

Documented proof of support includes evidence of payments to a child's caretaker (such as canceled checks or money orders), evidence of payment of child support under another child support order, and evidence of "in kind" payments (such as food, clothing, diapers, or formula that has been given a dollar value).

The available credit against gross income for either parent's qualified "not-in-home" children is the actual amount averaged to a monthly amount of support paid over the most recent twelve-month period to a maximum of 75 percent of a theoretical support order calculated according to these guidelines. None of these credits is available for stepchildren.

The third step, after calculating each parent's monthly adjusted gross income by deducting credits, is to take the amount of AGI each parent has, add them, and cross-reference the amount with the Child Support Schedule, which gives the monthly total obligation or BCSO both parents must provide.

The fourth step is to take the monthly BCSO and divide it by each parent's adjusted gross income. Each parent's share, called the percentage of income (PI), is determined by prorating the BCSO between parents. More steps follow.

Parenting Time Adjustment

The parenting time adjustment is an adjustment to the BCSO based on parenting time. In equal parenting situations, the adjustment is based upon each parent exercising 182.5 days, a half year, of parenting time.

Except as applied to equal parenting situations, the adjustment is based on the ARP's number of days of parenting time with the children. Only one parent can take credit for parenting time in one twenty-four-hour period. A "day" of parenting time occurs when the child spends more than twelve consecutive hours in a twenty-four-hour period under the care, control, or direct supervision of one parent or caretaker. The twenty-four-hour period need not be the same as a twenty-four-hour calendar day. Accordingly, a day of parenting time may encompass either an overnight period or daytime period or combination of these.

Except in extraordinary circumstances, partial days of parenting time that are not consistent with this definition shall be considered a "day" under these guidelines. For example, let's say an ARP picks up a child after school three or more days a week and keeps the child until eight in the evening. The three days of routinely incurred parenting time of shorter duration may be added up and counted as a single day for parenting time purposes.

More Time with Children

If the alternative residential parent spends ninety-two or more days per calendar year with a child, the assumption is that he or she is making greater expenditures on the child during parenting time for costs such as food and/or is paying child-rearing expenses for items that are duplicated between the two households such as beds and clothing. A reduction to the ARP's child support obligation may be made to account for these transferred and duplicated expenses.

The amount of the additional expense is determined by using a mathematical formula that changes according to the number of days the ARP spends with the child and the amount of the BCSO. This mathematical formula is called a "variable multiplier."

Conversely, parents who have parenting time less than sixty-eight nights will have to pay an increased amount of support due to the other parent's increased expenses.

"Split parenting" can occur in a child support case only if there are two or more children of the same parents, where one parent is the primary residential parent for at least one child and the other is the primary residential parent for another. Split parenting situations are calculated differently under the new child support guidelines so that both parents are given credit for having more than 50 percent of the time with at least one child.

Health Care Costs and Add-Ons

Under the child support guidelines the cost of medical insurance premiums (which can include dental insurance) that provides health care for the children and the costs of work-related child care are included in the calculation for the support order. The parents must divide these expenses according to each parent's percentage of income, and every court order under the guidelines must address these expenses.

As for uninsured medical expenses, they are added to the BCSO. These expenses must be routinely incurred so that a specific monthly amount can be reasonably established and added to the BCSO. Parents must divide these expenses according to their percentage of income regardless of whether they are routinely incurred and added to the BCSO. Uninsured medical expenses may include deductibles, co-pays, dental, orthodontic, counseling, psychiatric, vision, hearing and other medical needs not covered by insurance.

After calculating the BCSO and adding health insurance costs and work-related child support expenses, educational expenses for private or special schooling for children can be considered as a deviation from the presumed amount of support. The court may consider other special expenses such as music lessons, summer camps, travel, and other activities that may contribute to the child's cultural, social, artistic, or athletic development as deviations from the child support order and added to the child support amount.

These add-on expenses are not mandated under the child support guidelines and must exceed 7 percent of the BCSO to create a deviation before they're added to the BCSO.

Paying Child Support

Keep in mind that the guidelines are minimum requirements. Child support can be set above the guidelines' minimum requirements when warranted. One such instance could be a hardship deviation. Specific rules apply to a very narrowly defined hardship exception.

Courts can order an employer to deduct child support from the supporting parent's salary and pay it directly to the receiving parent. This is called a wage assignment. In Tennessee, the court should order it unless there is a good reason not to. This works extremely well. However, if the supporting parent is self-employed and gets much of his or her income in cash or is on a straight commission without a draw, this process might not be helpful.

A supporting parent may be ordered to pay child support through the state's collection agency. In many cases such payments simplifies the process for the custodial parent, who need not enter into confrontations with the supporting parent or use the children as collection agents. The agency maintains the record of payment, and when a parent fails to pay child support, the proof of the amount is much easier to obtain.

If the supporting parent moves out of state, the child support order may be enforced through both states' collection agencies. Armed with your state's court orders, you can go to the other state's court (often handled through the local district attorney or your local juvenile court) to enforce the wage assignment.

Child support is owed even if the supporting parent files for bankruptcy. Also, child support payments are not taxable income for the recipient parent or deductible by the paying parent. If your former spouse is not making child support payments after filing for bankruptcy, check with your lawyer immediately for advice.

Parents can agree to allow the parent paying child support (the ARP) to have the benefit of child dependency deduction as long as the recipient parent (PRP) completes and signs IRS Form 8332, which must be filed with the ARP's tax return. This is addressed in the permanent parenting plan form.

Ending Child Support and College

In Tennessee, the obligation to pay child support ends when a child reaches eighteen or graduates from high school with his or her regularly scheduled class, whichever comes second. However, child support could end earlier if the child becomes emancipated (gets married or quits school and gets a job).

Child support may continue after a child goes to college but only if the parties agree or if the child suffers from a severe medical condition or is handicapped. Otherwise, the court cannot order support past the age of majority or college tuition. But the court can order parents with substantial income to pay money into a trust for college and other extraordinary educational expenses, including educational travel.

Income Determination Challenges

When a parent's income cannot be ascertained, the child support guidelines read:

> When establishing an initial order and the obligor fails to produce evidence of income (such as tax returns for prior years, check stubs, or other information for determining current ability to support or ability to support in prior years), and the court has no other reliable evidence of the obligor's income or income potential, gross income for the current and prior years should be determined by imputing annual income

of $36,369 for male parents and $26,989 for female parents.

After the initial order, for situations in which the court has no reliable evidence of a parent's income or income potential, then the court shall enter an order to increase the child support obligation of the parent failing or refusing to produce evidence of income by an increment not to exceed ten percent (10%) per year of that parent's share of the basic child support obligation for each year since the support order was entered or last modified.

Self-Employed Parents

When a parent is self-employed, income can be different than that amount listed on the obligor's federal income tax return. According to the child support guidelines,

> Income from self-employment includes income from… business operations… and rental properties, etc., less ordinary and reasonable expenses necessary to produce such income....
>
> Excessive promotional, excessive travel, excessive car expenses, or excessive personal expenses, or depreciation on equipment, the cost of operation of home offices, etc., shall not be considered reasonable expenses.
>
> Amounts allowed by the Internal Revenue Service for accelerated depreciation or

investment tax credits shall not be considered reasonable expenses.

Fringe benefits for inclusion as income or "in kind" remuneration received by a parent in the course of employment, or operation of a trade or business, shall be counted as income if they reduce personal living expenses.

Such fringe benefits might include, but are not limited to, company car, housing, or room and board. Variable income such as commissions, bonuses, overtime pay, dividends, etc. shall be averaged over a reasonable period of time consistent with the circumstances of the case and added to a parent's fixed salary or wages to determine gross income.

Voluntarily Underemployed or Unemployed and Getting Behind

When the person owing a duty of support is voluntarily under-employed or unemployed, the court may order that parent to seek employment and report periodically with a diary of efforts to find work and to participate in government job search, training, or work programs. Every able-bodied person has an earning potential. Failure to pay child support can result in a petition for contempt, seeking incarceration for failure to pay court-ordered support. Depending on the situation, however, the unemployed obligor may seek a temporary reduction in support while seeking employment.

If a parent voluntarily takes a cut in income or quits a job, is child support reduced? That depends; the judge will have a lot of discretion in this situation. Technically, if a supporting parent is willfully and voluntarily unemployed or underemployed, child support shall be calculated based on a determination of potential income based on the obligor's educational level and/or previous work experience.

In this situation, though, individual circumstances matter. For example, if a doctor leaves one practice to start his or her own, the temporary reduction in income will not likely justify a reduction in child support. If, however, a manager of a retail store takes a new job with a cut in pay but also with legitimately increased advancement opportunities, the court might allow a decrease. On the other hand, leaving a job just to reduce hours or to intentionally make less money in order to pay less child support will not be looked upon favorably by the judge and can result in a child support obligation based on the obligor's potential income.

There are many appellate decisions discussing willful and voluntary unemployment and underemployment. If this situation concerns you, consult an experienced family lawyer.

In Tennessee, parents may not get out of paying past-due child support. The Tennessee child support statute mandates that child support immediately becomes a judgment when it is due and not paid. The law does not allow a reduction in past child support that has not been paid. Ask your lawyer, however, about provisions that may apply if a parent has completely interfered with visitation. In addition, if requested by a parent or required by a court, the court may add 12 percent interest.

Caps and Presumptions in "High Income" Cases

There is also a cap on child support as a certain percentage of income when the presumptive child support order exceeds the amount found by multiplying a net income of $10,000 by the percentages set out below. The primary residential parent seeking support in excess of the capped amount must prove that more than the capped amount is reasonably necessary to provide for the needs of a child. The court can order the excess be paid into an educational trust. The guidelines allow the following caps or percentages:

- One child (21 percent) = $2,100
- Two children (32 percent) = $3,200
- Three children (41 percent) = $4,100
- Four children (46 percent) = $4,600
- Five or more children (50 percent) = $5,000

The Tennessee Court of Appeals has approved several rulings awarding child support in excess of the cap for education, extracurricular activities, and educational travel for high-income obligors.

Retroactive Support Owed

In paternity cases, retroactive support may be ordered from birth and can include reasonable birth-related medical expenses. The court may also award child support retroactively to the date of separation of a married couple, abandonment of a child, or physical custody of a parent or non-parent care-taker. Retroactive support is calculated using the average income of the parties over the previous two years. Other provisions may apply if a parent has intentionally hidden a child to prevent visitation.

More about Private School Tuition

In *Barnett v. Barnett*, the Supreme Court of Tennessee held that private school tuition was an "extraordinary educational expense" that must be added to the obligor's percentage of child support computed under the child support guidelines. The court concluded that the guidelines consider private school tuition to be an extraordinary expense because private school tuition exceeds the cost of public schooling and should consequently be added to the obligor's percentage of child support computed under the guidelines. The court stated that this is equitable because there are some obligor parents who are substantially less well-off than custodial parents and that the imposition of private school tuition on these obligor parents would produce an extreme inequality to the amount of the obligor's contribution to child support.

Know that the child support guidelines categorize private school tuition as an "add-on." Look for a judge to balance all interests. Certainly, judges usually look for ways to limit the impact of divorce on children. Keeping children in the same school is important for the sake of continuity. On the other hand, judges do not want to order parents to pay for private school tuition if they can't afford it. An important fact for most judges is whether the parties paid for private school tuition prior to the breakup. If so, judges are very likely to try to figure a way to keep children in their existing schools.

Chapter Takeaways:

- Study Tennessee's child support guidelines. Details matter. Links to the guidelines are available at MemphisDivorce.com.
- Maximize the amount used for the other parent's income. Make sure all earned and passive income is included. The definition of gross income is very broad and can include untaxed income.
- Maximize your parenting time with your children when negotiating the permanent parenting plan.
- Make sure the costs for certain categories of your children's expenses such as health insurance premiums and child care are accurate. If you don't know the amount, find out from the source and anticipate future cost increases.
- Think about all the extra expenses your children may need such as tutoring, sports, and educational travel—now and in the future. Share those expenses with your lawyer and discuss specific strategies.
- Run different scenarios. Using the child support calculator, input different income amounts and parenting time (both high and low) for the variables and see how different inputs impact the final amount. You may be surprised. If a particular point in dispute has only a small impact on the outcome of child support, don't fight over it.

6

Alimony and Attorneys' Fees

Alimony always causes concern right from the beginning. Understandably so. Spouses know that alimony is going to be a difficult issue. For experienced family lawyers, alimony and attorneys' fees are often the last two pieces of the divorce puzzle. Before they get into advice on alimony and attorney's fees, lawyers want to know how all the other pieces fit. Hence the order of the chapters of this book.

Rarely do any divorces proceed in order because there is no real order. But from a number-crunching and financial-analysis perspective, family lawyers want to first identify all assets and debts, classify them as marital or separate property, and value them. Depending on the complexity of the marital estate (because it can include such things as pensions, stock options, real property, and investments), coming up with solid evaluations of assets and debts may take time.

At the same time, family lawyers figure out the income or earning potential of the parties and all monthly expenses, which allows them to narrow parenting time and child support obligation to a likely range. Finally, alimony and attorney's fees are tackled. This is another example of why the "one step at a time" philosophy is discussed throughout this book. There is no simple formula for working through alimony because it depends on so many other factors.

For example, let's say two couples have been married for twenty-four years each. Both supported spouses have college degrees and have not been employed outside the home for over ten years. But one supported spouse will receive assets over $2,000,000 and the other will receive net assets of about $200,000. Even if both supported spouses receive the same amount of child support, the types, length, and amount of alimony can be completely different.

Spouses naturally focus their attention on the questions of how much and how long because those are obviously important questions. But in Tennessee, the first question should be "What type of alimony will be awarded and why?" There are four types of alimony in Tennessee: transitional alimony, alimony *in futuro* (also called periodic alimony), rehabilitative alimony, and alimony *in solido*, and all of these are discussed below.

Then there are the factors for determining alimony, including the lifestyles the parties enjoyed during the marriage and their projected lifestyles after the divorce. After consideration of the likely types of alimony, their respective purposes, and maybe some legal research, experienced family lawyers will begin have some idea of the amount and length of payment may be negotiated.

In 2011, the Supreme Court of Tennessee issued *Gonsewski v. Gonsewski* (350 S.W.3d 99 [Tenn. 2011]), a landmark decision in which Tennessee alimony law was summarized and developed. Some lawyers have commented that it dramatically changed the direction of Tennessee alimony law that should lower the expectation of spouses seeking support. Not all lawyers agree that it made any significant difference; some think that the opinion only served to give family lawyers more direction on the type and emphasis of evidence presented at trial.

In *Gonsewski*, the Supreme Court of Tennessee denied alimony to a supported spouse because of the lack of evidence that the wife needed support. Below is a synopsis of the *Gonsewski* opinion, including a number of quotes from it, that provides an excellent summary of the history of alimony, the four types of alimony and their respective goals, the factors courts are to consider when awarding alimony, and evidence not presented in this particular case. This is an edited version of the opinion with legal citations omitted to help make it easier to read:

Alimony *in Futuro*

Alimony *in futuro* is intended to provide support on a long-term basis until the death or remarriage of the recipient. This type of alimony can be awarded where "the court finds that there is relative economic disadvantage and that rehabilitation is not feasible." Alimony *in futuro* is appropriate when "the disadvantaged spouse is unable to achieve, with reasonable effort, an earning capacity that will permit the spouse's standard of living after the divorce to be reasonably comparable to the standard of living enjoyed during the marriage, or to the post-divorce standard of living expected to be available to the other spouse." Alimony in futuro "is not, however, a guarantee that the recipient spouse will forever be able to enjoy a lifestyle equal to that of the obligor spouse." In many instances the parties' assets and incomes simply will not permit them to achieve the same standard of living after the divorce as they enjoyed during the marriage. While enabling the spouse with less income "to maintain the pre-divorce lifestyle is a laudable goal," the reality is that "[t]wo persons living separately incur more expenses than two persons living together... Thus, in most divorce cases it is unlikely that both parties will be able to maintain their pre-divorce lifestyle." It is not surprising, therefore, that "[t]he prior concept of alimony as lifelong support enabling the disadvantaged spouse to maintain the standard of living established during the marriage has been superseded by the legislature's establishment of a preference for rehabilitative alimony."

Alimony *in Solido* (or Lump-Sum Alimony)
Alimony *in solido* is also a form of long-term support. The total amount of alimony *in solido* is set on the date of the divorce decree and is paid either in a lump-sum payment of cash or property or in installments for a definite term.

"A typical purpose of such an award would be to adjust the distribution of the parties' marital property." Alimony *in solido* "may be awarded in lieu of or in addition to any other alimony award, in order to provide support, including attorney fees, where appropriate." Unlike alimony *in futuro*, the other form of long-term support, alimony *in solido* is considered a final judgment, "not modifiable, except by agreement of the parties," and does not terminate upon the death or remarriage of the recipient or payor spouse.

Rehabilitative Alimony

In contrast to alimony *in futuro*, rehabilitative alimony is intended to assist an economically disadvantaged spouse in acquiring additional education or training that will enable him or her to achieve a standard of living comparable to the standard of living that existed during the marriage or the post-divorce standard of living expected to be available to the other spouse. Rehabilitative alimony thus serves the purpose of assisting the disadvantaged spouse in obtaining additional education, job skills, or training as a way of becoming more self-sufficient following the divorce. This purpose is markedly different than the purpose of alimony *in futuro*, which is to provide long-term support when the economically disadvantaged spouse is unable to achieve self-sufficiency.

Transitional Alimony

Transitional alimony is appropriate when a court finds that rehabilitation is not required but that the economically disadvantaged spouse needs financial assistance in adjusting to the economic consequences of the divorce. Simply put, this type of alimony "aid[s] the person in the transition to the status of a single person." It is "bridge-the-gap alimony" designed to "smooth the transition of a spouse from married to single life." In contrast to rehabilitative alimony, which is designed to increase an economically disadvantaged spouse's *capacity* for self-sufficiency, transitional alimony is designed to aid a spouse who already possesses the capacity for self-sufficiency but needs financial assistance to establish and maintain a household without the benefit of the other spouse's income. As such, transitional alimony is a form of short-term support. Transitional alimony is payable for a definite period of time and may be modified only if the parties agree to it, the court provides for modification in the divorce decree, or the recipient spouse resides with a third person following the divorce.

Purposes of Alimony

The statutory framework for spousal support reflects a legislative preference favoring short-term over long-term spousal support to rehabilitate a spouse who is economically disadvantaged relative to the other spouse and to allow him or her to achieve self-sufficiency when possible. Thus there is a statutory bias toward awarding transitional or rehabilitative alimony over alimony *in solido* or *in futuro*. While this statutory preference does not entirely displace long-term spousal support, alimony *in futuro* should be awarded only when the court finds that economic rehabilitation is not feasible and long-term support is necessary.

The Factors for Awarding Alimony— What Courts Must Consider

Finally, in determining whether to award spousal support and, if so, determining the nature, amount, length, and manner of payment, courts consider several factors:

1. The relative earning capacity, obligations, needs, and financial resources of each party, including income from pension, profit sharing, or retirement plans and all other sources
2. The relative education and training of each party, the ability and opportunity of each party to secure such education and training, and the necessity of a party to secure further education and training to improve that party's earnings capacity to a reasonable level
3. The duration of the marriage

4. The age and mental condition of each party
5. The physical condition of each party, including but not limited to physical disability or incapacity due to a chronic, debilitating disease
6. The extent to which it would be undesirable for a party to seek employment outside the home because that party will be custodian of a minor child of the marriage
7. The separate assets of each party, both real and personal, tangible and intangible
8. The provisions made with regard to the marital property
9. The standard of living of the parties established during the marriage
10. The extent to which each party has made such tangible and intangible contributions to the marriage as monetary and home-maker contributions, and tangible and intangible contributions by a party to the education, training, or increased earning power of the other party
11. The relative fault of the parties, in cases where the court, in its discretion, deems it appropriate
12. Such other factors, including the tax consequences to each party, necessary to consider the equities between the parties

Although each of these factors must be considered when relevant to the parties' circumstances, "the two that are considered the most important are the disadvantaged spouse's need and the obligor spouse's ability to pay." Carefully adhering to the statutory framework for awarding spousal support in terms of awarding the correct type of support and for an appropriate amount and time fulfills not only the statutory directives but also alimony's fundamental purpose of eliminating spousal dependency where possible.

In *Gonsewski*, the Supreme Court of Tennessee concluded its analysis, stating:

"We are persuaded that alimony in futuro should not have been awarded in this case... Here, Wife has a strong earnings record through the course of the marriage." But then the court gave spouses and their family lawyers the following roadmap regarding evidence that needs to be presented:

- "[W]hat, if anything, Wife could or could not do to alter her earning capacity to permit her standard of living after the divorce to be reasonably comparable to the standard of living during the marriage."

- "No evidence was presented regarding the prospect or feasibility of Wife making any 'reasonable effort'" to alter her earning capacity.

- "Moreover, little evidence, other than their income and expense statements, was presented concerning the parties' standard of living during the marriage—whether lavish, frugal, or somewhere in between."

- "Nor was evidence presented regarding the post-divorce standard of living expected to be available to Husband."

This roadmap is very important. In a Tennessee divorce, both spouses should be prepared to submit evidence on earnings history and capacity, the possibility of vocational rehabilitation, and their lifestyles. A lifestyle analysis describes the parties' actual earnings history, projected earnings, actual or estimated spending history, and projected spending into the future. Learn more about what a lifestyle analysis is and how it is used at MemphisDivorce.com.

Negotiating Alimony

Working out what type of alimony, its length, and its amount is right for your situation is part art and part science. Figuring out what makes sense is one of the most important roles your attorney performs. Setting goals is very important. What will your budget look like in the future? How much can really afford to pay? Or how much do you really need? If you don't know, you may want to enlist the services of a financial advisor to help you and your lawyer.

Most experienced family lawyers welcome working with a divorcing spouse's financial advisor, especially if the marital estate is complex. The process of setting financial goals and budgets is a challenging process. A spouse's overall financial picture *today* is usually not that difficult to piece together, but getting an accurate look into the future can be very challenging. Property division and debt division may be somewhat predictable. From there, if child support applies, that amount may be calculated within a certain range. The rest is a budgeting exercise. What will be needed is judged against what income ranges exist. After the divorce, financial advisors can help with the transition.

If you do not have a financial advisor, your lawyer can almost always recommend one or more. These services are often provided for a flat fee or may be based on assets to be managed in the future. Even if you think your estate is not large enough, you will often be surprised by how much it is when you sit down and actually add it all up, and you can also be surprised how little it can cost to have it professionally managed. The benefits of making smart, well-informed decisions almost always outweigh the cost of making poorly informed decisions when negotiating alimony in divorce.

Short-term marriages are treated differently than longer term marriages. Here are some fictional examples:

- Paul and Sarah married a year after graduating from the University of Tennessee at Knoxville. They separated after seventeen years. Paul earns $165,000 per year as a manager in a major engineering firm. Sarah, a teacher, earns $32,000 per year and will be primary residential parent to their three children ages nine, fourteen, and sixteen. At mediation, Sarah accepted Paul's offer to pay her $2,250 per month transitional alimony for eight years in addition to child support and Paul's agreement to pay for each child's college tuition, room and board, books, and fees equivalent to that amount charged by the University of Tennessee for in-state tuition.

- John and Mary, a couple from Cordova, Tennessee, have been married five years. Near the beginning of their marriage Mary quit school so John could become a dentist. After finishing dental school, John found a new love and filed for a divorce. Because the marriage was of short duration, a court must first try to put the parties back in the position they were in before the marriage. Obviously, John has benefited from Mary's sacrifice. A court might award Mary rehabilitative alimony for two to five years to help her complete her college education and get her back on her feet.

- Steve and Jenny, a couple from Bartlett, Tennessee, have been married for twenty-five years and are getting divorced now all the kids are grown. Jenny started and owns an accounting firm, and she earns well into six figures. Steve teaches music at a high school and was the primary caregiver for the children. It may not be feasible for Steve to start over by going back to school. A court might award Steve alimony *in futuro*. Steve will receive a check until Jenny dies or Steve dies or remarries or receives support from a live-in relationship.

- Brad and Susan are both stockbrokers from Brentwood who make about the same income and have no children. Their largest asset is their home, which has equity of $180,000. Unfortunately neither has enough cash to pay the other for his or her share of the home. Brad might offer to pay alimony *in solido* each month until the one half of the equity in the marital home is paid so that he may keep the house. If Susan accepts this type of alimony, she cannot petition the court to increase the amount after the divorce because alimony *in solido* cannot be modified.

In divorce settlement negotiations, disputes involve the type of alimony, the amount of alimony, and length of time payments are to be made. Other considerations may include under what circumstances the alimony may be modified or terminated. Experienced attorneys' opinions vary about alimony. In deciding how to advise a particular client, attorneys consider the alimony factors listed above, prior experience with the judge and the other attorney, and case law.

Case law is legal jargon used to describe appellate opinions, opinions that result from prior cases having gone to trial and one party, being dissatisfied with the result for any number of reasons, appeals the trial court's ruling. The Court of Appeals rules on the issues raised by the appealing party, sometimes reversing the ruling of the trial judge, and issues a written opinion. Anywhere from one to five detailed alimony-specific appellate opinions are issued each month by the Tennessee Court of Appeals. When a dispute arises over what constitutes a fair amount of alimony, some family attorneys may research case law and look for a case that closely mirrors the particular divorce their dealing with and come up with a position that one party should be awarded more or less alimony. Even though there have been many cases decided by appellate courts, most situations are unique.

For many, transitional alimony will be an attractive settlement option because of its certainty and predictability. Although no formal statistics have been compiled on the matter, transitional alimony is likely the most popular form of alimony negotiated in settlements. Like most aspects of family law, negotiating alimony is again part art and part science. The skill and experience of family lawyers play a very important role in the process. Having a deep understanding of Tennessee law helps set the stage for this very difficult negotiation.

Attorneys' Fees

Attorneys' fees are unique in every case. Some spouses may agree to pay some of the other spouse's attorney's fees as part of the divorce settlement just to help make the settlement happen, while other spouses absolutely refuse to pay a dime. Some judges are apt to award them at trial, but many are not.

In general, there are two very different statements of Tennessee divorce law regarding attorneys' fees judges try to balance and lawyers struggle to explain. If there are enough assets awarded a spouse in the divorce from which he or she can pay attorney's fees, there should not be a separate award of attorney's fees. On the other hand, if the trial court finds a supported spouse needs those assets to live on and cannot afford to use those assets to pay attorney's fees, a court may award attorney's fees. Reconciling these two different points of law can be difficult for even experienced family law attorneys.

If there is a divorce trial, a trial court awards attorney's fees as part of alimony, and this means the alimony factors discussed above apply. Tennessee law places a great deal of discretion in the hands of the trial judge. Tennessee's Court of Appeals will rarely award them as part of the divorce if the trial judge refused to award them or awarded only a fraction of the fees charged by one of the parties' lawyer. Even though the Tennessee Court of Appeals will rarely overturn or reduce the trial court's award of attorney's fees if the trial court awarded fees, it does happen every now and then.

There are some cases in which courts are more likely to award attorney's fees. For example, there are cases in which judges perceive that one spouse fought needlessly tooth and nail. Judges may be more inclined to grant fees if one spouse lied to the court and got caught. If one party appeared to be completely unreasonable in his or her demands or requests from the court, the court is more likely to award fees to the other spouse. But when a judge thinks that there were tough issues that could have gone either way, he or she is not likely to award attorney's fees simply because the two parties needed the judge to decide difficult issues.

Very few cases go to trial solely on the issue of attorneys' fees because the trial itself may be more expensive than simply negotiating a settlement. But if one spouse is being unreasonable, there are times that trial cannot be avoided. Knowing the difference often requires relying upon the advice of your attorney.

Chapter Takeaways:

- Read and study Tennessee's factors for alimony in divorce. Share with your lawyer every important fact and piece of evidence, good or bad, applicable to the factors. Your lawyer needs information. Alimony negotiation is part science and part art.

- Maximize your spouse's income. Income determination is key. Does your spouse make more money than what appears on tax returns? Is your spouse paid cash under the table? Is there deferred compensation or stock options? Learn everything you can. If income determination is particularly complicated, consider hiring a forensic accountant to consult with you and your lawyer.

- Know exactly how much money you need to live on. Prepare a very detailed budget from reviewing your actual expenses. Estimate future needs. Consider working with a financial advisor as part of your divorce team.

- Learn what a lifestyle analysis is and how getting one can help your Tennessee divorce case. If helpful, consult with a forensic accountant or financial advisor. Read about lifestyle analysis in detail in the alimony section at MemphisDivorce.com.

- If either spouse needs retraining to become fully employed or increase earnings, he or she should consider consulting with a vocational expert or career counselor. Increasing earning capacity through additional education or retraining can make a big difference in a spouse's ability to pay support or can reduce a spouse's claimed need for support.

- In negotiations for alimony, it may be more expensive to go to trial than to pay the attorney's fees at stake.

7
Mediation and Collaborative Divorce

Mediation and collaborative divorce are two different things. Collaborative divorce is discussed in detail below. Most Tennessee judges require divorcing parties to attend mediation before a trial is held. Mediation is voluntary process led by a mediator. Almost all experienced family lawyers recommend spouses attend mediation with a lawyer, and most strongly recommend against attending mediation without one. Some mediators may disagree with those two statements, but if they do, they are wrong. Mediation is a great process. But the mediator cannot tell you what is best for you even on simple, basic issues. And there are some basic legal propositions you must be aware of. If you don't know them, you could really get hurt.

For example, if one party will receive the marital residence in the divorce, the other party should be relieved of the obligation to pay the mortgage. This usually means the spouse receiving the house must refinance the house. Without such a provision there should be no agreement. A mediator might not be able to advise a spouse to require the house be refinanced because that may be financially detrimental to the other spouse. If the divorce is settled, one spouse can end up owing money on a house he or she doesn't own. Having a lawyer helps you prevent these types of pitfalls.

Three functions performed by attorneys include investigating, negotiating, and eliminating variables. As you can imagine, negotiating a divorce settlement can be an emotional and legal minefield. There are a number of unfair negotiating tactics and strategies known by most family law attorneys. Having your attorney explain to you in clear, concise, and simple terms that the other spouse may be "testing the waters" with an overly aggressive negotiating position (and how to tactfully respond to it) can be one of the most valuable services your attorney can provide.

In most cases mediators are lawyers or former judges, although a law license is not required for mediators. Almost all mediators have been formally trained and can refer to themselves as "Rule 31" mediators. Although there are many mediators who have not practiced as family lawyers, most experienced family law attorneys will recommend mediation with lawyers for many reasons. One important reason is that lawyers who practice family law are much more familiar with Tennessee divorce and family law and its application to particular situations.

While it is common for one spouse to be perceived as "weaker," the mediation process is designed to prevent a stronger spouse from taking advantage of any perceived imbalance of power. Your lawyer can help advise you through the mediation process. Also, an ethical and experienced mediator will take this into account.

At mediation, spouses may (and should) have attorneys present. All experienced family lawyers are comfortable working within the mediation process both before and after divorce cases are filed. Your lawyer should help you make sure the agreement is fair, reasonable, and consistent with your financial goals. In theory, mediators are not supposed to offer any advice as to whether the terms of any agreement are fair or reasonable or comment on what a particular judge might order in the event of a trial. That is the role of your lawyer.

In Tennessee, if children are involved, mediation is mandatory. Even if the spouses have no children, most judges order both parties to mediate divorce even over one or the other spouse's objection. However, the mediation process is 100 percent voluntary. This is understandably confusing. If you are ordered to mediate, it does not mean you are ordered to reach an agreement, but the judge will expect you to show up and enter the mediation process in good faith.

Mediation is a form of alternative dispute resolution, a term that describes new procedures used by the courts to facilitate settlements. The theory is that many cases can be resolved without a trial if there is a formal process by which the parties meet to discuss the issues in the case. The process is controlled by Supreme Court of Tennessee Rule 31, and here are some of its provisions:

Section 1. Application
Pursuant to the provisions of this Rule, a court may order the parties to an eligible civil action

to participate in an alternative dispute resolution proceeding in accordance with this Rule.

Section 2. Definitions

(c) "Mediation" is an informal process in which a neutral person, called a mediator, conducts discussions among the disputing parties designed to enable them to reach a mutually acceptable agreement among themselves on all or any part of the issues in dispute.

(e) "Non-binding arbitration" is a process in which a neutral person or a panel, called an arbitrator or an arbitration panel, considers the facts and arguments presented by the parties and renders a decision which is non-binding.

(f) "Case evaluation" is a process in which a neutral person or a panel, called an evaluator or evaluation panel, after receiving brief presentations by the parties summarizing their positions, identifies the central issues in dispute as well as areas of agreement, provides the parties with an assessment of the relative strengths and weaknesses of their case, and may offer a valuation of the case.

Section 3. Initiation

Upon motion of either party, or upon its own motion, a court, by order of reference, may order the parties to an eligible civil action to participate in a judicial settlement conference, mediation, or case evaluation.

Section 4. Evidence

Evidence of conduct or statements made in the course of court-ordered alternative dispute resolution proceedings shall be inadmissible in court to the same extent as conduct or statements are inadmissible under Tennessee Rules of Evidence 408.

Section 6. Confidentiality

A Rule 31 dispute resolution neutral or settlement judge shall preserve and maintain the confidentiality of all alternative dispute resolution proceedings except where required by law to disclose the information.

Section 9. Participation of Attorneys

Attorneys may appear with clients during alternative dispute resolution proceedings.

Appendix A. Standards of Professional Conduct for Rule 31 Mediators

(4) The Mediation Process

(a) Orientation Session. On commencement of the mediation session, a mediator shall inform all parties that the process is consensual in nature, that the mediator is an impartial facilitator, and that the mediator may not impose or force any settlement on the parties.

(b) Continuation of Mediation. A mediator shall not unnecessarily or inappropriately prolong a mediation session if it becomes apparent that the case is unsuitable for mediation or if one or more of the parties is unwilling or unable to participate in the mediation process in a meaningful manner.

(5) Self-Determination

(a) Parties' Right to Decide. A mediator shall assist the parties in reaching an informed and voluntary settlement. Decisions are to be made voluntarily by the parties themselves.

(b) Prohibition of Mediator Coercion. A mediator shall not coerce or unfairly influence a party into a settlement agreement and shall not make substantive decisions for any party to a mediation process.

(c) Prohibition of Misrepresentation. A mediator shall not intentionally nor knowingly misrepresent material facts or circumstances in the course of conducting a mediation.

(d) A Balanced Process. A mediator shall promote a balanced process and shall encourage the parties to conduct the mediation deliberations in a nonadversarial manner.

(e) Mutual Respect. A mediator shall promote mutual respect among the parties throughout the mediation process.

(8) Professional Advice

(a) Generally. A mediator shall not provide information the mediator is not qualified by training or experience to provide.

(b) Independent Legal Advice. When a mediator believes a party does not understand or appreciate how an agreement may adversely affect legal rights or obligations, the mediator shall advise the participants to seek independent legal counsel.

(d) Personal Opinion. While a mediator may point out possible outcomes of the case, a mediator should not offer a firm opinion as to how the court in which the case has been filed will resolve the dispute.

There are many benefits to mediation. You stay in control of the outcome. If you don't agree, there will not be a settlement. The main benefit is that there can be less conflict, which can result in a better long-term relationship with your ex. As well, this reduced conflict may mean a more peaceful breakup for the children. Finally, if mediation is successful, the overall cost will almost certainly be less.

There are only a few possible downsides to mediation. If your spouse is hiding assets, you may never know it unless you have full discovery (see chapter 2), and a forensic accountant reviews the financial documents and advises you and your attorney.

Preparation for mediation is the key. Spend time with your legal team. Think of the likely strategies to be employed by your spouse and his or her lawyer. Know what you want. Have all necessary information well in advance. Knowing what you want and what to expect will make you much more calm and confident.

Hopefully, well in advance of mediation you and your legal team will have assembled a complete list of marital assets, separate property, and values. For real estate, do you need an appraisal? For pensions, should you know the calculated estimated value of pension interests? Has your lawyer detailed the necessary pension elections? For alimony, do you know what type of alimony you want, the length, and amount? Do you know what your spouse's income really is? Has your lawyer or financial expert reviewed all the necessary tax returns and financial statements? Have you projected your future earnings capacity and expected financial needs on a monthly budget? Should you consult a financial advisor? Tax advisor? If so, don't procrastinate.

If you have children, have you a completed parenting plan *exactly* the way you want it? Have you run several child support scenarios? All experienced family lawyers know how to negotiate. The success of your final mediation strategy is dependent upon your lawyer knowing exactly what you want.

Is there a burning issue you want to discuss with your lawyer in detail? If so, call your lawyer well in advance and schedule an appointment. Your lawyer can't read your mind. Almost all experienced family lawyers will expect clients to tell them what level of preparation they want or expect. Don't be shy.

The final step may be preparing a mediation statement, a general term used to describe a document used to inform the mediator about the most important facts of the case, key legal issues, all assets, their values, debts, income, and expenses. Some important factual pleadings may be shared including the complaint, answer, interrogatory answers, and responses to requests for production of documents.

Additional documents may include key evidence including pictures, e-mails, text messages, or deposition excerpts. Effective mediation statements will focus attention on your case's strengths and downplay its weaknesses. Some lawyers may share this with the mediator and/or the opposing party, while others may choose to not to share that information and work off the other party's information.

Be careful about disclosing too much information. Even though there is a technical rule that information exchanged in mediation is confidential and cannot be admitted into evidence in court, the reality is that disclosing certain aspects of your case may give the other lawyer time to prepare for trial in the event mediation in unsuccessful. As well, certain aspects of your case can never be effectively hidden. Expecting some secrets to remain secrets may be only wishful thinking. Deciding what information to disclose is one of the most important strategic decisions of your pre-mediation planning.

At the mediation, be friendly, calm, and open-minded. Like any other negotiation, you are looking for any advantage no matter how small, but appearing to be reasonable and open-minded may be more important than being brutally honest about how you feel or what you want. Don't shout, argue, or appear to be an aggrieved, victimized, or angry spouse even if you are intensely mad at your spouse, the mediator, or the process itself. When in doubt, ask to speak with your lawyer in private. If things get tense, maintain your poise; this demonstrates a sincere confidence in your position and is a negotiating strength. This is an important time for important adult decisions.

Mediation can be very boring. Some mediations have the mediator spending time almost exclusively with the other spouse. That can be a good thing. One never knows if the settlement is going to get done until it's signed. Be prepared for long stretches of downtime.

Mediation can be physically and emotionally tiring. If you get tired, take a break. Eat some protein-rich foods. Maintain your blood sugar and watch your blood pressure. If you feel that you're losing your cool, let your lawyer know. Take a break or whatever it takes to maintain an even keel. Bring to the mediation whatever you need to help keep you centered and calm. Some bring books, while others view family photos on their iPhones. Some pray. If you are too tired to make sound decisions, let your lawyer know. It may make more sense to try again another day.

Finally, don't expect to win every point in the negotiation. Don't expect to feel vindicated; don't expect to feel satisfied. The resulting settlement does not have to be perfect for the negotiation to be successful. One important goal should be to get the details that matter most handled one way or another. Some trials won't result in all the important details being handled. Mediators often say that mediated settlements almost always result in a better financial situation for you than a trial, and in almost all cases that's true.

A successful mediation ends with a summary of the settlement in writing, signed by the parties, or a complete set of divorce documents including the marital dissolution agreement (MDA), permanent parenting plan (PPP), and child support worksheets (CSW) signed and ready for entry with the court. The more complete the set of terms the better. Even if one party tries to back out of the agreement, most courts will enforce the terms of the settlement if documents are signed.

Collaborative Law

Collaborative law is a form of alternative dispute resolution that was invented in the 1980s. Since its introduction in Tennessee, many family law attorneys in the state have advocated collaborative law as a substitute for traditional divorce. Divorce is typically an *"adversarial"* process; this means that each party hires a divorce lawyer to zealously protect his or her interests. Alimony, custody, division of assets, and child support are usually determined through litigation under the adversarial model.

Collaborative law follows a different framework. Parties who enter into the collaborative law process initially agree not to litigate. Each party hires an attorney trained in collaborative law to try to negotiate a settlement with the opposing party's attorney.

The collaborative law process begins when both parties and their attorneys sign a four-way agreement to enter into good-faith negotiations rather than litigation. The attorneys and the couple seeking divorce hold meetings to discuss the possibility of reaching a settlement. These meetings may take the form of informal discussions between the attorneys or joint conferences with everyone present. During the process of reaching a settlement, nonlegal professionals may be brought in to assist the parties.

Financial information is exchanged between the parties over the course of the collaborative law negotiations. In the adversarial process this exchange occurs through the process of discovery. The court compels both spouses to fully and accurately disclose all relevant financial information. In contrast, the collaborative law process calls for a voluntary exchange of documents and information. Neither spouse can compel the other to fully disclose any financial information.

Although both parties initially sign an agreement to negotiate in good faith, the settlement process may be ended at any time by either party for any reason. There is no requirement that either party continue to participate in the process. If one party desires to unilaterally terminate the negotiations because of a disagreement or a breakdown in communication, both attorneys and all hired professionals must withdraw from representation. Once a party decides to withdraw, both parties will have to hire new attorneys. From one perspective, all the money and time spent on the divorce process up until that point is lost. But if an agreement is reached, the parties sign settlement documents. These documents typically include agreements to dissolve the marriage, divide property, set custody schedules, and set child support payments. The documents are then submitted to the court for approval.

The Uniform Collaborative Law Act (UCLA)

Attorneys and professionals specializing in collaborative law have recently led a movement to establish uniform standards for its practice. The Uniform Collaborative Law Act (UCLA) was drafted in 2009 to promote uniformity in the practice of collaborative law. The UCLA sets forth specific rules and procedures meant to guide attorneys and professionals through the collaborative law process. The UCLA was designed so that state legislatures would find it easy to make it state law.

The UCLA may apply to areas beyond divorce law. The drafters of the UCLA had difficulty defining "family law," and thus the language of the act allows for the practice of collaborative law in non–family law situations. While proponents of the UCLA claim that 90 percent of all collaborative law practiced is family law, the act itself can be applied to all areas of the law.

The effort to promulgate the UCLA, however, has met limited success. In 2011, the American Bar Association's House of Delegates rejected a resolution calling for the approval of the UCLA. State-level attempts to enact the UCLA have also been unsuccessful. Although uniform standards have been proposed for enactment in almost every state, the overwhelming majority of state legislatures have declined to adopt the UCLA. As of 2011, only Utah, Nevada, and Texas had given legislative recognition to collaborative law. In 2010, the Tennessee state legislature failed to pass a bill that proposed uniform collaborative law standards. Although an increasing number of attorneys hold themselves out as collaborative law practitioners, there are still no requirements governing its practice in Tennessee.

Is Collaborative Law Right For Me and My Tennessee Divorce?

Because no set standards exist for the practice of collaborative law in Tennessee, it is vital that a spouse seriously weigh the options before choosing collaborative law over litigation.

One aspect of collaborative law is that a spouse's attorney is disqualified from further representation if a settlement cannot be negotiated. Many believe this motivates collaborative law attorneys to encourage the negotiation process. Parties may be able to avoid going to court if an agreement is negotiated.

There are other potential benefits to the collaborative law process. One benefit is that the collaborative law model holds a potential for decreased animosity between parents. If both parties are able to fully agree on custody arrangements and future child support payments, it can reduce stress on the whole family. Another benefit is that an outside expert, like a financial planner or a CPA, called a financial neutral, may be brought in to assist during the process. Although this expert adds to the overall cost of the divorce, he or she can save the parties from each having to hire a financial expert, which would most likely be more expensive.

There are, however, potential disadvantages. The major disadvantage of the collaborative law process is the possibility that the parties' entire investment in a collaborative law lawyer can be lost. If negotiations break down and either spouse decides to withdraw, the attorneys for both spouses are disqualified from all legal representation in the divorce. Essentially, one spouse has the power to fire the opposing spouse's lawyer. When one spouse withdraws, all the fees paid to the collaborative law attorneys and nonlegal experts may end up being completely wasted. If one spouse's funds are limited, the other spouse holds the power to place the financially disadvantaged spouse in a precarious financial and legal situation. Cleveland attorney and past American Bar Association Chair of the Family Law Section Marshall J. Wolf has noted:

> It does not matter that one party wishes to continue with the collaborative process, that party's lawyer is disqualified. It does not matter that the less economically advantaged party is financially burdened with the requirement that he or she must begin anew with a new lawyer who is precluded from receiving input from the disqualified lawyer or the disqualified lawyer's files and work product. In the event of a failure of collaboration, all is lost!

Furthermore, the collaborative law model provides little room to question the validity of the opposing party's financial statements and disclosures, while an attorney engaged in litigation has the ability to challenge and question the opposing side. Parties who do not fully and voluntarily disclose information during the litigation process may be compelled by the court to produce financial information under oath, but even though full and voluntary disclosure is encouraged under the collaborative law model, there is no formal procedure to compel a complete exchange of all financial information and documents.

An attorney who challenges the completeness or accuracy of the opposing spouse's disclosures runs the risk of upsetting or alienating the opposing spouse. This is dangerous because the opposing spouse can decide to withdraw from the negotiations at any point.

In addition, a violent or coercive relationship is not eligible for a collaborative law divorce. Both attorneys become automatically disqualified from representation if violence or coercion occurs after the spouses have agreed to enter negotiations. Even if the innocent spouse is abused or coerced, both spouses must seek new counsel.

Another potential disadvantage is the ethical challenge the collaborative law process can pose to lawyers. Attorneys have a duty to zealously represent their clients. The nature of collaborative law has led many attorneys and courts to question whether the process violates attorneys' ethical and professional obligations. As a 2005 New Jersey Supreme Court opinion stated, "The danger is that a lawyer committed to the collaborative law process may lack the capacity, even unconsciously, to provide a client with a fair representation of the risks and benefits of utilizing such a process."

As of 2012, the practice of collaborative law is not favored in Colorado. A 2007 Colorado Bar Association Ethics Committee Opinion noted that the practice of collaborative law presents a fundamental conflict of interest. Before negotiations, both attorneys must sign a contract in which they agree to withdraw from representation if negotiations end. This disqualification agreement means that one party's choice of counsel essentially rests in the hands of the opposing party. The opinion notes the following:

Even if the client's advance agreement is made "knowingly and freely," [withdrawal is permitted] only where it can be accomplished without "material adverse effect" on the client's interests. Where the client is of relatively meager means, the lawyer's withdrawal may be materially adverse to the client. Under such circumstances, the lawyer's withdrawal may be unethical.

The Colorado Bar Association found the collaborative law agreement to be a fundamental conflict of interest that could not be waived by the client.

Collaborative law is an alternative but risky substitute to traditional litigation. Both spouses should be fully informed at the beginning of the process if the collaborative law format is chosen. Anyone considering collaborative law as an alternative to litigation should seriously weigh the benefits and risks.

8

Divorce Strategies, Settlements, COBRA, and Taxes

Divorce Strategies

When you're going through divorce, you'll get a lot of great life advice you can soak in from many different sources. Some divorcing spouses spend a lot of time at their churches or synagogues and speak with their pastors, priests, or rabbis. Many read self-help books and talk to friends and family. Others take yoga classes or accept wisdom from the Dalai Lama or Deepak Chopra through Tweets. Take what you need. Leave the rest. Stay calm. Don't expect too much out of fortune-cookie wisdom found in any book or Internet site. If you are hurting, get professional help from an experienced mental health professional and begin your divorce recovery as soon as possible.

For great legal advice, stay focused. Assemble a great team. Hire an experienced family lawyer who is right for you (see chapter 13 for more advice on how to hire a family lawyer). and trust him or her to take your situation seriously. So if your Uncle Joe tells you something about legal aspects of divorce, be very skeptical. There are always exceptions to any legal situation. Listen to your lawyer. In addition, you may need a counselor, financial advisor, forensic accountant, business valuation expert, tax advisor, real estate appraiser, or appraiser of other types of property.

Two of the biggest variables in any divorce are your judge and opposing counsel. Never underestimate the importance of either, especially in divorces with children. All parents raise their children differently. While many judges are parents and grandparents, some aren't. And opposing counsel can also present a different set of parenting biases. Some lawyers have very detail-oriented type-A personalities while others are the "Let's get it done at the last possible minute" types. All these variables can affect the settlement terms of your divorce.

You don't have to be perfect to be successful in your divorce; you simply need to avoid making major mistakes, and you can do that by reading, listening, and learning as much as you can. This book is written to help you start that process. The more you read and learn in the beginning of your Tennessee divorce, the more likely you will avoid pitfalls.

Very Best Divorce Strategies

- Tell the truth. Credibility is vital. If you lose credibility with your judge, you can lose every part of your Tennessee divorce.

- Understand there is often no such thing as "winning" a divorce, but you can certainly lose a divorce.

- Pay attention to Tennessee's statutory factors. For property division, child custody, and alimony, Tennessee law provides lists of factors courts must use to determine outcomes in every divorce. Even if your Tennessee divorce case eventually settles, being prepared to present your case along the lines of those factors will help you negotiate from a position of strength. Share with your Tennessee divorce lawyer every important fact and piece of evidence, the good and the bad, applicable to the factors. They are your "cheat sheet."

- Communicate. Keep your legal team informed of important developments. Provide the requested documents and information in a timely fashion. Ask a ton of questions. Lawyers can't read your mind. The only stupid question is the one you didn't ask that your divorce lawyer assumed you knew the answer to already.

- Get off Facebook and other social media. Whatever you do, don't assume that none of your "friends" will share with your spouse what you post. As a vindictive response, your spouse may become angrier and refuse to settle, even on reasonable terms.

- With your Tennessee divorce lawyer develop your action plan. Focus time and effort on your important objectives, and then work your plan. When disputes arise that don't impact your overall objectives, don't fight over them; save arguing for important matters.

- Take care of *you*. Eat right. Exercise. If you need to get some professional counseling, do so. Don't drink to excess. Get enough sleep. It's okay to say "no" to others right now, including your friends and parents and those asking you to volunteer time at your children's school or your church. When you are done with your divorce, you can make it up to everyone.

More Important Divorce Strategies

If you suspect your spouse is cheating, hire a private detective but—very important—only after talking to your lawyer. Get to your doctor immediately and have tests for sexually transmitted diseases, and then go back in six months or whenever your doctor suggests to be tested again.

Never joke about harming your spouse, even among friends, in texts, e-mails, or otherwise.

Never let anyone take "fun" photos or videos of you in a bar hugging an old friend from grade school, and don't let others post images of you on their own social media. Judges expect you to act more conservatively during divorce, not like a frustrated parent reliving his or her *Animal House* college days.

If your spouse leaves abusive voice messages or sends you threatening texts, save them and get them to your lawyer as evidence.

Avoid emotional highs and lows. In times of stress, your feelings will lie to you. Rarely is your case as strong as you may think. At other times, rarely is your case as weak as you may feel.

Even if you really hate your spouse's lawyer, don't say anything about him or her. That might give your spouse information that can be used against you. Plus, divorce lawyers have thick skin and are accustomed to being told awful things the client's spouse said, and some even may enjoy it. Even if you think your lawyer is better than your spouse's lawyer, don't count on that winning your case. In court, the facts of your case can be much more important than the skill of the lawyer.

In divorce, just as in life, control is an illusion. No one controls the case except maybe the judge. But even the judge does not have the power to dictate the terms of a settlement—the parties do, and settlements require both sides to compromise.

Grab documents as soon as possible. Examples of papers the attorney will need are federal and state income tax returns (including copies of W-2s), pay records for the current year, financial statements, employment contracts, explanations of benefits, and all canceled checks and credit card charge records for at least the last twenty-four to sixty months. Be sure to make copies of anything that might be important before it disappears. See chapter 12 for a more complete list.

Document everything. Write down details of your spending. Keep canceled checks and all monthly statements. Keep a log of all child support, alimony, or other temporary support paid or received.

Pet custody issues are always difficult. In most cases divorcing spouses usually ultimately reach a compromise, although pet disputes are on the rise nationally. There are occasions where courts have ordered pet visitation after divorce. In determining who will get the pet, courts will look at the children's primary residence, whether the pet was a gift, who was the original purchaser, and who was the primary caregiver and/or paid for food and vet bills.

Once you've engaged a lawyer, tell him or her all the awful stuff about you. Most of the time, when a client is afraid to tell a lawyer something unfavorable to the client's case, it turns out to be something not to fear or to be manageable if given prompt attention. Waiting until the last minute to talk about a problem can cause bigger problems. It's better to plan for the monster in the closet together than to wait and see the look of shock in your lawyer's eyes when the monster emerges.

When in doubt, be friendly to your spouse. When a soon-to-be-former spouse asks a tough, direct question, just be calm and find a way to delay your response. Call your lawyer, discuss the situation, and then respond. A thoughtful response may prevent your spouse from setting unreasonable expectations.

Before your lawyer can advise you, he or she must have all the facts. Many times, the lawyer will ask a client to write down everything that is or even might be important. Writing this "novel" can be a therapeutic experience for the client. Some lawyers read fast and digest written information more easily. Also, tell the lawyer about any and all suspicions. For example, "My spouse took a trip to Orlando last spring and didn't take the children." This could lead to important deposition questions under oath inquiring whether anyone accompanied your spouse.

Set aside time to "work" on your divorce. A divorcing spouse needs to collect important documents, read the material the lawyer provides, and explore divorce recovery options such as counseling, recovery groups, and self-help books on coping and financial advice.

Almost all experienced family lawyers consider one attorney representing both parties in a divorce a serious conflict of interest. Ethics mandate attorneys to honor the highest degree of loyalty. But if a lawyer represents two parties, which client receives the higher degree of loyalty?

In divorces where only one party is represented, the unrepresented party who is waiting to hire an attorney only after signing a divorce settlement might be undertaking the ultimate adventure of rearranging deck chairs on the *Titanic*.

When one party violates a court order, the court can enforce the order after the harmed party files a petition for contempt that asks the court to order the violating party to serve time in jail or pay money. This can be emotionally painful and expensive. Try to work out small differences. Problematic situations may require the lawyer's attention.

Never call your spouse's lawyer. If you are represented, the lawyer cannot talk to you because it is unethical. If you are not represented, the lawyer shouldn't want to talk to you because the lawyer should be afraid you might claim you received legal advice. If your spouse's lawyer ever calls you, immediately tell your lawyer.

Never threaten or brag. Whether out of a sense of desperation or whether you feel a moment of clarity, never predict the future. Certainly, never make such statements in e-mails or texts. They don't intimidate, and they won't make you feel better; at worst, your own words will be used against you in a future court hearing.

Settlements

Let your lawyer negotiate the divorce. Experienced family lawyers negotiate for a living. Every lawyer has his or her own negotiating strengths, weaknesses, style, experience, and preferred strategies and tactics. Understand the negotiating strategy for your case. Be on the same page. Communicate. Work together.

In divorce settlements, the divorcing parties may not always get what each deserves, but each party will get what is negotiated. Feeling comfortable that your attorney has your best interests in mind may be the most important factor in trusting your lawyer and strategy. Without trust, communication usually breaks down. While maneuvering through the legal minefield of divorce, if you make a decision against the advice of your attorney, do not be surprised by the sounds of explosions.

In your divorce settlement, if you have a choice among receiving $50,000 in a money market savings account, $50,000 in Disney stock, or $50,000 in an IRA, which should you choose? In most divorces cash will likely be the most important asset you can receive. Cash means liquid assets such as money in checking and savings accounts, CDs, and traditional money market accounts.

In order to liquidate stock and real estate, divorcing spouses receive assets with the tax basis at the time of the divorce. There may be a built-in capital gain taxes owed on stock appreciation making that $50,000 in Disney stock worth less than its potential sales value.

In general, retirement assets are more important only to those spouses with enough cash to need to defer taxable income. So in this case of $50,000 in an IRA, there will be no taxable income until the IRA starts getting distributed. The appreciation will be taxed, however, at the time of distribution during the retirement years. But cash can be placed in investments that do not result in taxable interest such as municipal bonds. For financial and tax advice about your specific situation, consult with your CPA or financial advisor.

For jointly owned real estate, only four options exist in divorce settlements:

1. the wife buys out the husband
2. the husband buys out the wife
3. the parties sell the real estate and split the proceeds
4. the parties own the property jointly after the divorce

Keep in mind that in a settlement agreement calling on one spouse to pay a debt that's in both parties' names, if the party responsible for the debt does not pay it, the other party can still be liable for it.

If a spouse will be giving up mortgaged real estate that was jointly owned, he or she should consider requiring the other spouse get preapproved refinancing for it in his or her own name prior to signing any divorce settlement.

Since the recession, at least one Tennessee judge has required refinancing preapproval before approving a divorce settlement that requires one spouse to refinance jointly owned real estate.

Only two roads exist to getting a divorce: settlement or trial, and there can be many sources of delay. Frequently one lawyer is generally waiting on the other to produce documents, respond to a settlement offer, or just return a phone call or letter. This waiting can shift back and forth several times during a case. Another source of delay occurs when the parties are waiting for a court date setting or a decision. Avoid delays whenever possible.

A family lawyer does three things for a living: communicate, negotiate, and eliminate variables. Keep in mind that the lawyer cannot read minds. The lawyer does not always know how much the client knows or wants to know. If you think that your question is important, it is. Ask it.

Moving On

Don't remarry the day a divorce is granted. The court ends a case by signing a final order. Once the final order is "entered" in the court's docket, an appeal period of thirty days begins to run. After that appeal period runs, the divorce is finally final. Few situations could be worse than getting married the day after the judge signs the final order only to find out a week later that the former spouse appealed the case.

Remember that after a divorce you'll need to change your will and update the beneficiaries on your life insurance policies. You should seek out the advice of an estate planning attorney who can work with your financial advisor. Your experienced family lawyer can refer you to attorneys and financial advisors.

You might not think you have a large enough estate to need the services of a financial planner, but once you sit down and add up all your assets, you may be surprised. And there are many competent financial advisors willing to help you plan and build your financial position regardless of how much money with which you may start!

What should a divorcing spouse do about moving on with one's life? Getting a divorce is very painful. One of the best books available is not a divorce book but a book about changes in life: Gail Sheehy's *New Passages* for women, and *Men's Passages* for men. These are not a self-help books filled with happy talk but serious discussions of a collection of life stories about real, professional and educated men and women moving through life's stages, including divorce, death of a spouse, cancer, and job loss. Discovering that feeling anger, shame, loneliness, or guilt is shared by others going through life's changes can help you to face important issues that come and go during and after a divorce.

If you are sad, realize you may find yourself willing forgive those who have hurt you the most. You must also forgive yourself. This takes time. If you are angry at your spouse, never try to exact revenge in the divorce process. Like most situations in life, the best revenge is living a successful life after divorce. How you decide what is successful is completely within your control.

Extending Health Insurance Coverage—COBRA

The Consolidated Omnibus Budget Reconciliation Act of 1986 (COBRA) is a federal law that allows eligible employees and/or dependents (spouse and children) who are losing their health or dental benefits to continue coverage in certain circumstances where coverage might otherwise end. Qualified beneficiaries may be eligible to continue coverage for a specific length of time following certain qualifying events, but not all employers offer COBRA benefits.

Through COBRA, individuals pay the entire monthly premium plus an administrative fee and may be able to remain insured with their health plan for a certain length of time up to thirty-six months. Continuation of health insurance coverage can be one of the most important issues in a divorce especially if one or more of the parties involved have preexisting medical conditions.

But because federal and state laws can and do change, if there is an important point that needs to be determined for certain, let your lawyer know so that the proper advice can be obtained in advance of the problem needing to be solved. Don't wait until the last minute!

In general, individuals may have as few as thirty days from the date of the COBRA notification letter to complete and return the application to the employer. To be eligible for COBRA, individuals must already be participants in a group health or dental program. COBRA participants may add new dependents within sixty days of the date the dependent is acquired. Any past-due premiums may be due within a short time period, say forty-five days after the initial application is signed. COBRA premiums may not be prorated. Coverage can be terminated automatically and cannot be reinstated if the correct monthly premium is not paid by the end of the month. Check the employer's specific restrictions and requirements because they may differ among employers.

Divorce and Taxes

Prior to filing divorce, you do not need to have a good grasp of the tax impact of your decisions, but when a divorce settlement is proposed, you'll absolutely need the advice of a tax professional—a CPA or tax lawyer. Some very important and complex tax implications may be involved that could have a huge financial impact on your future, especially if you have a larger or a more-complicated marital estate. Rarely are the tax implications spelled out in the settlement paperwork. Federal income tax law determines what taxes may be owed, not Tennessee divorce law. Divorcing spouses can be responsible for the resulting tax liability sometimes in spite of what a settlement may spell out or not spell out.

Family lawyers rarely have the expertise to give tax advice because tax laws can change almost every year. Almost all experienced family lawyers will refer you to a tax professional. But here is a very short list of pointers and tips:

IRS Publication 504—Divorced or Separated Individuals is a great place to start if you want to look up a tax question. And it's free over the Internet at www.IRS.gov.

The filing status you choose depends partly on your marital status on the last day of your tax year. If you are unmarried, your filing status is single, or, if you meet certain requirements, head of household or qualifying widow or widower. If you are married, your filing is either married filing a joint return or married filing separate return.

Generally, there is no recognized gain or loss on the transfer of property between spouses or transfer of former spouse's income.

Child support cannot be deducted by the party paying it, and it is not considered income by the party receiving it.

In general, a payment to or for a spouse under a divorce or separation settlement agreement may be deducted by the party paying it and considered the income of the recipient if the spouses do not file a joint return with each other and all the following requirements are met:

- The payment is in cash.
- The divorce settlement does not designate the payment as not deductible to the payor.
- The spouses are not members of the same household at the time the payments are made.
  (This requirement applies only if the spouses are legally separated under a decree of divorce or separate maintenance.)
- There is no liability to make any payment (in cash or property) after the death of the recipient spouse.
- The payment is not treated as child support.

In general, legal fees and court costs for getting a divorce are not deductible. But you may be able to deduct legal fees paid for tax advice in connection with a divorce and legal fees you pay in the process of getting alimony payments. In addition, you may be able to deduct fees you pay to appraisers, actuaries, and accountants for services or to provide a reasonable child support allowance in determining your correct tax or in helping to get alimony. Talk with your CPA and take advantage of any opportunities for deductions.

Very stringent and complicated rules govern taking advantage of a child's dependency exemption. For the spouse with whom the child does not reside to claim the deduction, there are specific rules including the execution of IRS Form 8332 by the primary residential parent and filing that form with the claiming spouse's tax return.

WARNING: In tax law there are exceptions and exceptions to exceptions. All experienced family lawyers encourage divorcing spouses obtain professional tax advice from a CPA or other tax professional.

9
Electronic "Snooping"

Taping Telephone Calls, Reading E-mails, Wiretapping, and GPS Devices

Privacy laws have been and will continue to in the news. Society wants to protect privacy. Even older laws, such as federal and state criminal laws, have been enforced more than ever. Know that other states' laws may apply as well. Some are much more restrictive. As technology advances, so will the opportunities for electronic snooping. If it was ever on your computer, assume it can be retrieved. Embarrassing videos, photos, e-mails, and Internet history are all fair game and not that hard to retrieve. Know that in Tennessee, placing a GPS tracking device on your spouse's car may be a crime.

The unmistakable conclusion is that you must discuss with your lawyer any plans you have to make recordings, etc., of your spouse. In general, the potential benefits of such evidence are almost always outweighed by the risks. If you want to engage the services of a private investigator or computer expert, discuss this first with your family lawyer. If you violate privacy laws running your own investigation, the evidence you may uncover may not be admissible in court. Or, even worse, you may find yourself charged with or accused of a crime.

The Electronic Communications Privacy Act (ECPA), enacted in 1986, updated the Federal Wiretap Act of 1968, which did not address the type of technology available today. It intends to prohibit the intentional interception, disclosure, or unauthorized access to the private electronic communications of others.

An example of an intentional interception would be monitoring your spouse's conversations in an Internet chat room or placing a wiretap on the telephone to listen to a conversation. An example of unauthorized access to a private electronic communications would be accessing your spouse's private e-mail account and reading the stored messages.

There must be a justifiable expectation of privacy accompanying the communication in order for there to be a violation of the ECPA. For example, an e-mail account carries with it a justifiable expectation of privacy, whereas posting a note on a bulletin board, electronic or otherwise, does not. The ECPA prohibits only unauthorized interception, disclosure, or use. If you have received the consent of your spouse to access his or her e-mail account, for example, this would not be a violation of the ECPA because your use is not unauthorized. The consent may be expressed verbally or in writing or implied. However, if a password, for example, is given to you for a specific purpose, you may not use the password for any other purpose because this could be a violation of the ECPA.

The Tennessee Wiretapping and Electronic Surveillance Act is similar to the ECPA as in it imposes penalties for intentionally intercepting, disclosing, or accessing without authorization the private communications of another individual. Attempting to, endeavoring to, or procuring another person to intercept or access communications is also a violation of the act, which considers violations to be Class D felonies. A person injured may recover in a civil action the greater of: 1) The sum of the actual damages, including any damages to personal or business reputation or relationships, suffered by the individual and any profits made by the violator as a result of the violations; or 2) statutory damages of $100 per day for each day of violation or $10,000, whichever is greater; and 3) punitive damages, reasonable attorney's fees, and other litigation costs incurred. The injured individual may also seek injunctive relief to restrain such violation along with the action for damages.

10
Testimony Tips for Depositions, Hearings, and Trials

A spouse going through divorce can testify at a deposition, a temporary support hearing, a pretrial motion, a petition hearing, or a trial. Here are a few basic tips. Your lawyer can provide you with more advice specifically tailored to you and your situation.

Depositions

Your deposition may be taken for many reasons:

1. Opposing counsel wants to find out what facts you know and don't know. In other words, your spouse's lawyer wants to hear your story.

2. Opposing counsel wants to pin you down to a specific story so that you will have to tell that same story at trial.

3. Opposing counsel may hope to catch you in a lie. From deposition to trial, the opposing counsel may try to figure out how to prove you lied at a deposition in order to show that at trial.

4. Some questions are simply designed to get your background facts established. These questions are boring, tedious, routine, and almost always necessary. The fastest way to get through with the deposition is to relax and answer the questions. Your lawyer may ask even more tedious questions of your spouse!

At your deposition, the other attorney can and should ask you the names of witnesses who may know facts and observed events in your marriage, parenting, and divorce. If the witnesses you mention testify differently from what you say at the deposition, your opposing counsel can try to use that difference to undermine or impeach the believability of your testimony at the hearing or object to certain witnesses because their testimony was a surprise.

You may also be asked about grounds for divorce and fault as a factor for alimony. These questions may require you to say awful things about your spouse. Be thoughtful and careful. Don't exaggerate, embellish, or equivocate. If your spouse hit you, say so. If you cheated, be honest. Talk to your lawyer about specific strategies on grounds and fault.

Don't bring papers with you to the deposition, especially notes from your lawyer. If you reviewed them to prepare for the deposition (or your testimony at trial), you may be required to give them to your opposing counsel. If you need to see copies of pleadings in your case, your lawyer should have copies.

Think of your deposition as a dress rehearsal for trial. Your performance may have an impact on settlement negotiations. If your spouse expects you to fall apart and cry, stay cool as a cucumber. If you spouse expects you to get angry and spit in your spouse's lawyer's face, stay cool as a cucumber. Keeping a cool head may be all that's needed to convince your spouse to settle on your terms.

Don't chitchat with the opposing lawyer or party before, during, or after depositions or hearings. Remember, your opposing counsel is your legal enemy. Do not let his or her friendly manner cause you to drop your guard. If your opposing counsel is menacing to you, don't act scared. Appear attentive but indifferent and unaffected.

Preparing for Your Testimony

Dress conservatively, even in a boring fashion. Avoid trendy and flashy attire with bright colors. If you have questions about what clothes to wear, have your lawyer check them out in advance for preapproval. Conceal tattoos. Remove piercings. Put your best foot forward. Show respect for the court and the proceedings regardless of how you may actually feel about them. Choose your court clothes well in advance. Get them ready the day before court knowing you may be nervous the morning of court. For depositions you should dress "business casual."

For court, dress professionally and tastefully, as if you were going to church. Men should always wear a suit jacket, a tie, and little jewelry other than a watch or a simple ring. Women should wear as little makeup as possible and very little jewelry. Never wear tennis shoes, T-shirts, shorts, sexually suggestive attire, or any jewelry or pendants that make political or religious statements.

Well in advance of trial your attorney will prepare you for court and share with you certain basics of testifying. Let your lawyer know how you feel and what level of preparation you think you need. Some clients are very comfortable and need very little "coaching," while others may want a great deal of preparation. Rarely is court as exciting or threatening as people imagine it to be. If you are still very nervous, ask your lawyer if you should attend court for other cases just to watch.

Be sure to tell your lawyer if you think you might have a problem. For example, if you think you might get angry, your lawyer can work with you and can share techniques to avoid problems. If you lose your temper, you may lose your case.

If you are asked to meet at the courthouse, know the name of your judge or chancellor, whether it is Circuit or Chancery Court, the number of the division or part, and what floor your courtroom is on. Consider driving to the courthouse a day or more before your court appearance and learn where to park, assuming the closest parking lots may be full. Taking steps like these in advance can help reduce stress before your day in court, and that's always worth the effort.

Normally you may invite a support person, such as a friend or parent, to accompany you in court. Talk to your lawyer before you bring your child even if your child is an adult.

Arrive at least fifteen minutes before court is scheduled to begin so that you will have additional time if parking or traffic is difficult. When you get to the courtroom, if you do not see your lawyer immediately, just find a seat. If the courtroom is full, or if you're uncomfortable sitting in it for any reason, sit just outside the courtroom within eyesight of the door.

Call your lawyer the day before a court appearance or a deposition because scheduling can change at the last minute for many different reasons. Confirm that the hearing or deposition is still scheduled, and ask any last-minute questions. Take a long walk and get a good night's sleep the day before depositions or court, and eat a sensible breakfast that gives you enough energy but not so much that you feel weighted down. Pack a couple of food bars in case you get hungry, and remember to bring along pain relievers and any medicine you normally take that will not make you drowsy or affect your ability to testify completely and truthfully.

Testimony Tips

Tell the truth—it's much easier to remember. You want to be perceived as a credible and truthful witness. They are calm, confident, polite, thoughtful, patient, responsive, alert, and assertive. Calm witnesses are credible witnesses. Deceptive witnesses are defensive, evasive, sarcastic, impatient, and disrespectful, and they tend to exaggerate, argue, and be quick to anger.

Judges and chancellors should be addressed as "your honor." Never argue with anyone—that's what you pay your lawyer to do. If you think you've given an incorrect answer, at any time you can ask the court to allow you to go back to a prior question so that you can correct your testimony.

Listen carefully to every question. Pause before answering. Make sure you understand the question, think about it and your answer, and then be direct with your answer. Answer only the question asked of you—then stop talking. Do not add any commentary. Pause just a bit before answering so your lawyer has an opportunity to object to questions if he or she thinks that's necessary. If the judge says "objection sustained," you do not need to answer the question. If the judge responds "overruled," you must answer the question.

When testifying in court, speak directly to the judge. Know that the judge may ask questions as well. Be sure the judge can hear you easily. Don't shout, but understand that some judges may have difficulty hearing soft voices in large rooms. Speak slowly and clearly. Do not nod or shake your head in response to a question or say "uh huh" or "nuh, huh." The court reporter must hear your answer in order to record it.

Do not worry about silence. The other lawyer may be thinking of the next question. Do not be tempted to fill the silence with words. Keep quiet and wait, even if the other lawyer is staring at you, implying that you are not finished answering the question, as if to say, "Keep talking." Do not fall into this trap. Just look at him or her calmly and politely as if to say "I'm waiting on you to ask another question."

Another common tactic is for a lawyer to ask you if you have discussed your testimony with your lawyer. This is asked in a manner calculated to imply that you have been coached or have been told what to say. The correct response is to say: "Yes." If asked what you were told to say, your response can only be "The truth."

Even if you really dislike the other attorney, never show it. If you do it will almost certainly be misinterpreted. If the opposing attorney tries to cut you off, be patient. You will be allowed to explain your answers. And know that if you give testimony that is not favorable and need to explain your answers further, your attorney will likely have a chance to ask those questions of you in a redirect examination.

If you do not understand a question, ask for the question to be repeated. Lawyers often ask confusing questions, but they are usually not intended to be confusing. If you think you are speaking too fast, stop, pause for a second or two, slow down, and then finish your answer. Always keep in mind that you are not in a conversation. The regular rules of human interaction do not apply. If you are not certain about the meaning of a word, don't be embarrassed; ask the lawyer to define it. Don't attempt to help the questioner by saying, "If you mean this, then my answer would be…"

Be sure you hear and understand the question. If the questioning lawyer lowers his or her voice or a noise in the room prevents you from hearing every word, ask to have that particular question repeated. You are not being impolite.

Regarding nerves, know that it is natural to feel nervous. Appearing nervous will not make you appear less truthful. Know that your lawyer is in charge. Take a deep breath. Put one foot in front of the other.

Compound questions ask two questions in one sentence: "Did you ever see your spouse do such and such, and if so, what was your reaction?" is an example. Answer only one question at a time. If you are confused by a complicated or multipart question, ask to have it repeated and clarified.

When you are being questioned, do not routinely look at your lawyer. "Looking for help" will indicate to the questioner she or he has touched on a sensitive area.

Never joke or make sarcastic statements in the courtroom or at depositions. Humor is not apparent on a transcript and may make you look crude or cavalier. For example, in divorce depositions, sexual preference questions are not unusual. In one case a wife answered a question sarcastically, "Yes, I'm a lesbian," and laughed in such a way to make it clear that she was obviously being sarcastic. Unfortunately, the transcript has no way to record sarcasm, and the result was an awkward statement that was later used in court to suggest she'd left her husband for another woman.

Do not fence or argue with opposing counsel. Opposing counsel has a right to question you. Do not answer a question with a question unless the question you are asked is not clear.

If you need a break, you can have one. Feel free to request a drink of water. Don't hesitate to request a recess of the proceedings if you are tired or if you need to use the restroom. If you must smoke, request a break. Remember, however, that when it comes time to go to court, you may not be able to have smoke breaks.

Chewing gum is not allowed in court. Don't do anything that will make it more difficult for the court reporter to understand you clearly and record your testimony accurately. Plus, chewing gum is generally viewed as disrespectful.

If you are shown documents, take your time and read them carefully and thoroughly. Look at the date, the author, the signature, the addressee, and to whom copies were sent. Don't assume you know what document has been shown to you.

If you are prepared for your testimony, everything will be okay. Your performance will not likely make or break your case. In most divorces, the facts, work history, and marital history have the greatest impact. This includes age, education, earning capacity, and track record as a parent. There is nothing you can do to change what happened in the past, so don't try.

If the judge rules in your favor, don't jubilate, smile, laugh, or react in any way. Your spouse will never forgive you for rubbing it in. If the judge rules against you, never groan, complain, cry, lament, or react in any way. Don't give your spouse the satisfaction. Stay poised. Don't even react outside the courtroom or even outside the courthouse. Your spouse may see that as well. Save your emotional response for when you're alone or with friends.

Finally, never brag or lament to your children or anyone who may later share what you say to your spouse. Whether you feel vindicated or victimized, prevent those feelings from being shared with children, even teenagers or young adults, because it still puts them in the middle. Assume that gloating or lamenting to friends and family members will get back to your spouse. Odds are you'll have some future event to share with your ex such as a child's wedding. Or your spouse may have the right to appeal. Never give your spouse added incentive to seek revenge against you.

Always remember that the divorce will eventually end and you'll be able to get on with your life. Take one step at a time. The best revenge is living a successful life after the divorce. How you define success in your own life is completely within your control.

11

When Professionals Divorce in Tennessee: Dividing Professional Practices

Professional Practice Valuation in Tennessee Divorce Law

Professionals who are partners, shareholders, or solo practitioners of a professional practice such as doctors, lawyers, dentists, and certified public accountants have consulted attorneys and accountants on the most advantageous ways to set up their practices, focusing on the twin issues of professional liability and tax liability. Smart planners may have already considered the consequences of divorce by prenuptial agreements or other pre-divorce planning devices. Most, however, have not.

If you're in a professional occupation such as the above and contemplating divorce, the most important thing to remember is *don't panic.* Underlying the obviousness of the advice is an important legal principle: undertaking asset liquidation or other moves outside the ordinary course of business can open up a spouse to the charge of "dissipation of marital assets," that is, taking assets out of the marital estate for the sole benefit of one spouse and to the detriment of the other.

Trying to manipulate assets during the breakdown of a marriage is also a good way to lose credibility with a court as the divorce winds its way through the legal system. Judges simply don't like spouses who try to hide or shield assets in ways that are not specifically sanctioned in the tax code. It is therefore important for professionals to continue to operate their practices without regard to impending divorces to the largest extent possible.

The Discovery Process in a Professional Practice Divorce

During the divorce process, the lawyers will engage in discovery to ascertain the marital estate, that is, all the assets acquired by the parties during the marriage. Just because a spouse started or joined a professional practice before the marriage, however, does not mean that none of the professional practice is part of the marital estate. Thus, the attorneys have the right to undertake discovery to determine the value of the professional practice both at the time of the marriage and at the time of divorce in order to determine what portion of the value of the professional practice is part of the marital estate.

In the discovery process, all financial records of the practice are open to scrutiny. This does not mean, however, that confidential patient information is also open to discovery. State statutes regarding confidentiality as well as federal Health

Insurance Portability and Accountability Act (HIPAA) will shield these records.

Valuing a Professional Practice

There are many reasons someone might need to value a professional practice: admitting a new partner or expelling an existing partner, the death of a partner, the purchase or sale of merging practices, estate planning, financing, interpartner disputes, and of course divorce. When a professional practice is valued for divorce, the method of valuation can differ from the methods used in other situations. For example, the partnership agreement may specify that in the case of one partner leaving the practice, "book value" will be used to determine each partner's share. This method of valuation, however, is not appropriate in divorces.

Moreover, professional practices, as opposed to other businesses, have special valuation issues that do not arise in other businesses, the most important of which are the concepts of "professional goodwill" and "personal goodwill."

Standards of Value

The first step in valuing a professional practice is to determine the standard of value to be used. There are a few generally accepted standards of value:

Fair market value is defined as the price a willing buyer would pay to purchase the asset on the open market from a willing seller, with neither party being under pressure to complete the transaction. In the divorce context, the court must find present net fair market value, i.e., fair market value reduced by the value of any liens or other debts that encumber the business as of the appropriate date of valuation. In Tennessee, assets are valued as of the date of the divorce, not separation.

Most courts agree that in reaching "net" fair market value, even though fair market value assumes a hypothetical sale, unless a sale is actually contemplated, it is inappropriate to deduct the costs of that hypothetical sale.

It is also important to note that the date of valuation is determined by statute of case law, which varies from state to state. It is therefore important to determine the appropriate date of valuation.

Liquidation value is defined as the amount the owner would receive if forced to sell the asset on the date of valuation. Liquidation value assumes a sale under compulsion, and almost always yields a value lower than fair market value. Courts have generally rejected liquidation value as a standard of value.

Going concern value is a broad term that comprises a group of standards of value that look to the value of the business as an ongoing, functioning enterprise. The distinguishing feature of going concern value is that it emphatically rejects liquidation value or book value.

Book value is defined as the value arrived at by adding all assets and deducting all liabilities. Book value is highly subject to manipulation and is thus generally not used by divorce courts as the standard. Many courts, however, consider book value as one piece of evidence in determining fair market value.

Original cost is the purchase cost of the business or the start-up cost of the business. Because most if not all professional practices increase in value after the initial costs of tangible assets are acquired, original cost is not an appropriate measure for a professional practice.

Other standards of value include replacement value, appraised value, investment value, and intrinsic value.

Of course, in the divorce context, the parties are free to agree or stipulate to the valuation of a particular business. Such agreements or stipulations are ordinarily binding on the parties in the absence of fraud, duress, overreaching, and other contract defenses.

Valuation Methods

Although the goal of valuation is to reach a determination of "present net fair market value," the courts do not require any one particular method of reaching that determination. The following are commonly accepted methods of valuing of a professional practice:

- IRS's Revenue Ruling 59–60
- Total Value Method

Under either of these methods the court adds the value of the physical assets and the accounts receivable and subtracts the liabilities.

Depending on which state law applies, if the business has divisible goodwill (discussed below), courts may also value the goodwill as a component of the practice's value.

Valuation of divisible goodwill has its own subset of valuation methods:

- Capitalization of Excess Earnings
- Comparable Sales
- Subjective Estimation

Under the capitalization of excess earnings approach, the court computes the difference between the actual earnings of the business and the earnings of the "average" business. This difference is then capitalized, i.e., multiplied by a factor of between one and five.

Capitalization of excess earnings is the most generally accepted valuation method where goodwill is divisible. If the business owner has deliberately depressed business earnings in order to minimize the value of goodwill, then this approach will yield an incorrect value. Thus dissipation should always be considered if goodwill is valued at zero.

Under the comparable sales approach, the person doing the evaluation looks at sales of similar businesses in the same area near the date of valuation. Goodwill is determined by subtracting the total sale price in comparable sales from the total value of tangible assets.

Some courts have accepted subjective estimations made by expert witnesses when those estimations are based on factors such as the practitioner's age, health, past earnings power, reputation, professional success, and other subjective factors such as whether the business is highly dependent on one customer.

Goodwill or Not Goodwill in Tennessee Divorce Law?

The first step in understanding the division of authority on the divisibility of goodwill is to define goodwill accurately. When businesses are bought and sold on the open market under conditions far removed from any divorce case, the negotiated sale price is often greater than the total value of the tangible assets of the business involved. This value is "goodwill," which Webster's defines as "favor or advantage that a business has acquired especially through its brands and good reputation." Because the definition of goodwill is based on the difference between the tangible asset value of a business and the actual sale price when it is sold on the open market, the question of whether a business can be actually bought and sold is crucial to determining the divisibility of goodwill. If the goodwill can actually be bought and sold, then it is realizable goodwill (sometimes referred to as "enterprise goodwill") and can be valued. If it cannot be bought and sold, the goodwill is unrealizable goodwill.

Realizable Goodwill

The easiest type of goodwill to classify is realizable goodwill: that which the owner can convert into cash at any time by selling his business on the open market. Where goodwill is readily convertible into a cash equivalent, the cases agree almost uniformly that it constitutes marital property that can be valued. Since realizable goodwill has an immediate cash value, it cannot be argued that it represents nothing more than future earnings.

It could, perhaps, be argued that the value of such goodwill is speculative, but the courts have generally held to the contrary. If increased future earnings are sufficiently likely so much so that buyers in arm's-length transactions are willing to pay an enhanced price, it is hard to argue that the increased earnings are so speculative as to make valuation impossible. As a Maryland court noted, "True goodwill reflects not simply a possibility of future earnings, but a probability based on existing circumstances."

South Carolina has held that all goodwill, including realizable goodwill, is not divisible marital property. In Tennessee, realizable goodwill, that is, goodwill that can be sold on the market, is part of the value of business. But this law will continue to change and evolve over time and may include case-specific determinations based on the type and size of the professional practice.

Unrealizable Goodwill

Division of goodwill is a much more complex issue when a business cannot be sold on the open market. This situation applies most frequently in the professional practices of doctors, lawyers, and mental health professionals in which the goodwill is indistinguishable from the personal reputation of the professional. In the case of unrealizable goodwill, nothing remains when the professional dies or retires. The professional's files and lists of clients may be of no use to others. The very nature of a professional practice is that is totally dependent upon the professional. The states are now almost evenly divided on the question of whether such unrealizable goodwill is divisible property. In Tennessee, the courts have held that unrealizable goodwill cannot be valued and divided in divorce.

Valuation Procedures

The most important witnesses in a complex valuation case will be the experts hired by each of the parties to value the business. Courts prefer well-qualified witnesses who know the particulars of the business to be evaluated and are able to clearly articulate their basis for the valuation. When an attorney understands the law and the valuation expert is able to render a persuasive opinion, the client has a winning team.

Other Valuation Issues
in Tennessee Divorce Law

While valuing the goodwill of the professional practice is the most tricky valuation issue when a professional divorces, other assets associated with the professional practice should not be overlooked. As noted above, the fair market value of the professional practice is the standard, and this includes tangible assets of the business as well as its accounts receivable and even contingency fees for work performed during the marriage. Retirement accounts, including 401(k)s, IRAs, and other employment-related vehicles are also valued and divided if they are marital property.

"Dividing" the Practice

Although divorce courts will "divide" the marital estate, a court will never "divide" a professional practice so that both spouses are owners (partners or shareholders) of the practice, and this is for two reasons: First, state laws prevent a nonprofessional from having an ownership share in a professional practice. Second, having spouses as co-owners of a business keeps the spouses' financial lives entangled, and one of the goals of divorce is to untangle them.

In Tennessee, a court will never order a professional practice to be sold and the proceeds split between the parties. Tennessee considers professional goodwill to be unrealizable and thus not part of the marital estate, but it still considers it of value to the spouse who is operating "the going concern." If a sale were forced, the sale price (fair market value including enterprise goodwill) would not equal the value placed on the professional practice by the party running it.

What the court will do is award the owning spouse the professional practice and either order the owning spouse to pay the non-owning spouse an amount representing the non-owning spouse's share (a monetary award) or grant to the non-owning spouse an amount of other marital property equal to the non-owning spouse's share (an offsetting property award). In Tennessee, the preferred approach is granting an offsetting property award.

If the marital estate's primary asset is a professional practice, the court might not order an offsetting property award if there isn't enough other property (for instance, savings or a vacation house) to offset the spouse's share of the value of the professional practice. In that event, the court may make a monetary award that is payable at a rate that pays off the award as soon as practicable. Monetary awards that take years and years may not be fair to the non-owning spouse even if the award has interest included.

No matter whether the court orders a monetary award or an offsetting property award, there should be no adverse tax consequences. Internal Revenue Code 1041 provides that a transfer of property between a husband and wife or a former husband and wife because of a divorce is a nontaxable transaction in which the recipient assumes the existing adjusted basis of the property and all liability for any capital gains tax if and when the property is sold after that point.

The tax consequences are not the same, however, if the owning spouse assigns income to the non-owning spouse as a means of paying a monetary award. An assignment of income is a taxable transaction, so there are tax consequences to both the assignor and the assignee.

To learn more-specific examples of how Tennessee courts handle different types of professional practices, see www.MemphisDivorce.com and its blog category on business valuation. There is also a helpful article on how to engage a business valuation expert.

12

Documents to Take to Your Lawyer[1]

Documents are the lifeblood of divorces. Spouses make choices every day that are documented in credit card statements, bank statements, tax returns, and many other records. Unless altered, documents don't lie. Documents tell the tale of those choices and are objective witnesses. Your family law attorney will need the documents listed below to adequately represent you in your divorce.

Before assets and debts can be divided they first must be identified, classified, and valued. Classification means determining what is separate property and what is marital property. In determining spousal and child support, courts look at what the obligor spouse (the one who must pay) earns, and that analysis depends in large part on the spouse's earnings history. Your spouse's income history may be reflected in the many pieces of paper gathering dust in closets and manila file folders.

When lawyers say "documents," they mean the paper copies (or hard copies), the electronic versions, or both. Today, almost all scanned documents will be in Adobe Acrobat's PDF format. For example, bank statements can be mailed to you, or you may download them online, usually in PDF format. But personal financial management programs such as Quicken or Quickbooks may generate reports of monthly income and expenses. These reports may be printed on paper or stored in PDF format. Your lawyer may prefer to have the electronic versions of these files, and he or she may even ask you to obtain a copy of the entire personal finance software program as well.

If you can easily obtain the hard copies and the electronic copies, get both. Save the electronic versions of the documents to a thumb drive, burn them to a CD, or e-mail them to your lawyer. Because making copies of voluminous documents can be costly, you may want to avoid copying. However, skip photocopying only if you are absolutely sure that the electronic versions are exactly the same.

Talk with your lawyer about who should make copies, handle the scanning, and/or organize the documents. Some lawyers encourage clients to copy and organize documents themselves in order to cut down on charges. Other family law attorneys will perform these tasks in order to handle them within their own document management system. Who copies, scans, and organizes documents often depends on the size of the estate and the complexity of the disputed issues.

Once you've gathered and assembled the documents, take them to your lawyer. Some clients wait too long, accumulating as many document as they can, before they bring in anything.

The next thing they know weeks have gone by. Don't be afraid to grab a bunch of documents, throw them into a box, and bring them to your lawyer's office. You can always make more than one trip. In some cases lawyers may want only a copy (or a scan) of the documents and ask you to replace them quickly so your spouse does not miss them. Speed is important.

Some documents contain important information that may not be apparent at first glance. Dates, times, places, amounts, payees, and other details may become terribly important later in the case. The values of assets at the time of marriage also may be important, especially if the marital or community property to be divided includes appreciation of separate property. Depending on your state's law, figuring out what amount is separate property may depend on the value of an asset as of the date of marriage, the date it was received in inheritance, or the date it was received as a gift. This means you may need documents going back in time as far as the date of the marriage.

For major documents such as financial statements, tax returns, and brokerage account statements you may want every single page you can put your hands on. For other documents such as those concerning a major acquisition of a business interest seven years ago, you may want documents going back around eight years. For less-valuable assets and debts, only three to five years' worth may be needed. It just depends. When in doubt, copy it. But before going to a great deal of expense or effort, talk with your lawyer. Getting the right answer to a quick question can save time and money.

Establishing Credibility

Memories fade with time. One particular number or date on one particular page among thousands can become very important if it validates your testimony or contradicts your spouse's testimony. In divorce, credibility is one of the most important aspects of any case. Once a judge determines a spouse's statements can't be trusted, recovering credibility can be very difficult.

You may need to download and print online banking and brokerage accounts from the Internet. If so, you may need a login name and a password. If you don't know them and your name is on the account, call the bank or brokerage firm and ask for help. If your spouse is a buddy of the banker or stockbroker, you may want to talk with your lawyer before calling to obtain that login information. Sometimes a call for login help and passwords can tip off the other spouse that a divorce is imminent.

Smoking-Gun Documents

Bring to your lawyer any information or documents that are potentially damaging to your case. Some clients pray the other spouse won't find a "smoking gun" document and go to great lengths to hide it amidst a mass of other documentation or simply won't produce it. This is a mistake. If you produce five years of credit card statements, hoping to bury one embarrassing statement in a stack of documents, the opposing attorney will almost always find it.

Likewise, if you omit a particularly damaging statement, the missing page may stick out like a sore thumb. If that page eventually gets discovered and turns out to list charges for an out-of-town trip with a previously undisclosed paramour, your own lawyer can be blindsided in negotiations or, worse, in court in front of the judge. Active concealment of documents—from your own attorney as well as from the other side—can destroy your credibility. Many experienced family law attorneys will tell their clients to assume that the other spouse will find out everything, so clients need to share with their lawyer everything damaging to the case. Only careful planning with your attorney can safeguard your credibility with the judge and minimize any potential embarrassment and/or financial costs of the divorce.

Following is a list of documents to obtain. Your spouse may receive similar instructions from his or her own lawyer. If a particular document is not listed below but looks important, include it anyway—it's always better to be safe than sorry.

1) **Prenuptial and postnuptial agreements**
2) **Financial statements**
   a) statements of net worth
   b) balance sheets
   c) income statements
   d) profit-and-loss statements
   e) statements of cash flow
3) **Income tax returns**
   a) state and federal
   b) W-2s
   c) 1099s
   d) K-1s
   e) supporting schedules

f) attachments, receipts, or schedules

g) depreciation schedules

4) **Pay statements**

5) **Bank account information**

    a) bank statements

    b) check stubs or registers

    c) deposit slips

    d) canceled checks

6) **Brokerage account statements**

    a) physical stock certificates or bonds

7) **Loan applications**

    a) personal and business financial statements

    b) any other documents showing why the debt was incurred

8) **Business ownership records**

    a) stock certificates

    b) charters

    c) corporate minutes

    d) operating agreements

    e) trusts

    f) joint venture agreements

9) **Resumes**

10) **Internet history, e-mails, and instant messaging records**

11) **Stock options**

    a) detailed plan descriptions or plan summaries

    b) benefit statements

    c) employment contracts

    d) schedules of vested and unvested granted stock options

        i) numbers of options

    ii) exercise dates

    iii) exercise prices

    iv) expiration dates

    v) vesting dates

  e) employment manuals

  f) brochures

  g) handbooks

  h) memoranda

  i) reload and replacement provisions

12) **Pension plans, profit-sharing plans, deferred compensation agreements, and retirement plans**

  a) all benefits statements

  b) most recent benefits statements

  c) summary plan description

  d) qualified domestic relations order (QDRO) procedures and sample forms

  e) full text of the plan itself, if available

  f) Booklets, pamphlets, information sheets

13) **Credit card statements**

14) **Other debts**

  a) name of the debtor and/or creditors

  b) date each debt was incurred

  c) total amount of the debt

  d) unpaid balance

15) **Insurance**

  a) policies

  b) declaration pages

  c) recent statements showing balances and premiums due

16) **Real estate**

  a) deeds

b) closing statements
c) appraisals
d) mortgages
e) security agreements
f) leases

17) **Personal property or "stuff"**
a) invoices
b) receipts
c) contracts
d) appraisals
e) photos of valuable assets

18) **Employment records, contracts, and explanations of benefits**
a) employment agreement
b) documentation of compensation
c) bonuses, commissions, raises, promotions
d) expense accounts and other benefits or deductions
e) employment handbook or manual

19) **Wills, living wills, powers of attorney, and trust agreements**
a) signed documents
b) statements, receipts, disbursements, and investments

20) **Membership agreements or contracts**
a) country clubs, private clubs, associations, or fraternal organizations
b) membership agreements
c) monthly dues statements

21) **Lawsuits and judgments**
a) copies of pleadings

    b) bankruptcies

    c) prior divorces

22) **Gifts and charitable contributions**

    a) nondeductible gifts

    b) gift tax returns

23) **Medical records**

    a) records documenting the diagnosis

    b) names of treating physicians

    c) evaluation reports

    d) prescriptions for medical, psychiatric, or psychological treatments

24) **Cellular phone, home telephone, and long-distance charges**

    a) detailed records of calls

25) **Inventory of safe deposit boxes or in-home safes**

26) **Tapes, letters, e-mails, and photos**

    a) text messages

    b) phone messages

27) **Notes or agreements**

28) **Calendars**

    a) personal and business

    b) computerized organizers

    c) smart phones

    d) personal daily assistants

    e) daily planners

29) **Intellectual property**

    a) royalties

    b) patents

    c) trademarks

    d) copyrights

30) **Fault**

Disputes over children

1) **Report cards and notes**
   a) notes from parent-teacher conferences
   b) improvement or decline in grades
2) **Cards, drawings, and sample photos**
   a) love, affection, and emotional ties shown in art or schoolwork
   b) handful of photos of the children enjoying daily living
   c) kitchen, bathroom, living room, and children's bedrooms
3) **Primary caregiver**
   a) food, clothing, medical care, education, and other necessaries
   b) notes setting regular dental appointments
   c) evidence of scheduling and driving the children to a tutor
4) **Continuity, stability, and community records**
   a) importance of continuity in your children's lives
   b) stable and satisfactory environment
   c) home environment
   d) school activities
   e) community involvement
   f) pictures of trophies or awards
   g) academic achievement, sports, church activities, or scouting
5) **Preference**
   a) preference of the children to live with one parent
6) **Abuse**

a) evidence of physical or emotional abuse
b) photos of bruises
c) medical records for doctors' visits
d) police incident reports
7) **Other adults**
a) evidence of the character and behavior of any other person who resides in or frequents the home of a parent
b) embarrassing Facebook photos
c) Match.com and other Internet dating listings
d) other parent's new boyfriend's or girlfriend's arrest records, bankruptcies, and lawsuits
8) **Family calendars**
9) **Homemaker**
a) showing the stay-at-home parent's involvement
b) children's special needs
c) religious education
d) home schooling

13
Choosing and Working
with a Lawyer

Many spouses thinking about divorce will procrastinate because they feel overwhelmed. Don't. As soon as you think there may be a divorce, you should interview two or three attorneys who practice family law exclusively. Some very important choices are made early in the process, and you need to make smart decisions now. Divorce changes everything—from temporary support to health insurance—and family lawyers have important advice to share.

Begin by researching lawyers. Talk to people you respect and trust. If you know a lawyer, ask for a referral. Always ask for referrals to lawyers who practice family law only. Most attorneys will agree to meet with you for a consultation. Many experienced family attorneys require a fee for such meetings.

Armed with several referrals, read the lawyers' Web sites, paying particular attention to his or her detailed professional biography. You want a lawyer with expertise in family law and a serious commitment to that particular legal field, and a lawyer who practices family law exclusively demonstrates that commitment. Family lawyers keep up to speed in their complex area of law by being members of the American Bar Association Family Law Section, Tennessee Bar Association Family Law Section, and other organizations specifically concerned with family law.

Subscriptions to monthly family law newsletters and books help lawyers track changes in the law. Without a specific commitment to family law, many lawyers who practice in other areas won't have the right reference material in their offices or access online. Every day the courts of appeal issue new opinions, and every year legislatures enact new laws. Child support guidelines are updated every three years or so, so keeping up isn't easy. Research any one lawyer's leadership and involvement with professional associations such as presenting seminars for judges, lawyers, and other divorce professionals, and check if they have published books and articles. Gauging a lawyer's leadership capabilities, public speaking experience, and history of publishing in family law is one way to objectively consider a lawyer's reputation and competence.

Watch out for lawyers who promote low-cost divorces. Keeping costs down is always good, but low costs can be a warning sign. Experienced family lawyers can tell horror stories about being asked to repair devastating legal problems caused by lawyers who made avoidable mistakes. But hiring a more expensive lawyer won't guarantee a better result either. You must do your homework.

Make calls and set up consultations. Expect the lawyer's staff to be professional and courteous. When you arrive at a lawyer's office, expect the lawyer to pay attention to you and to be patient and answer your questions. Expect the lawyer to be assertive without being arrogant. Trust your intuition. Run away from any lawyer who acts like you are lucky to be his or her client. Expect the lawyer to present himself or herself in a professional manner. The lawyer and the lawyer's office should not be a mess.

Chapter 12 offers a thorough list of documents your attorney will ultimately need, but for your initial consultation with your attorney it could be helpful to have your hands on important documents, including:

- Financial statements
- Income tax returns
- Bank statements (business and personal)
- Brokerage or retirement account statements

You have every right to understand what the lawyer says; even if your contemplated divorce involves complicated aspects of law. It's not a good sign if you don't understand what is being said.

Expect the lawyer to keep your children's best interest in mind. A custody fight can be more devastating to children than to the couple involved. Experienced and caring lawyers can teach you how to keep children out of the fray. Some lawyers may refuse to represent parents who are hell-bent on putting their children in the middle of the litigation's crosshairs.

Expect the lawyer to have a policy for returning calls, and some will even have their policies in this matter in writing. Ask to see it and read it. If a lawyer's clients are unhappy, the most likely reason is that the lawyer continually failed to return calls and keep them updated.

Even though you should not feel you are personal friends with your lawyer, you should expect to feel comfortable on a professional level. Expect the lawyer to interview you too. Don't be offended. You want a lawyer who is selective in taking cases. For a number of important reasons, better family lawyers are not interested in representing everyone. Just like you may not feel comfortable with the lawyer, the lawyer may not feel comfortable with you. That's okay. If that happens, don't take it personally.

Expect the lawyer to be up-front about who will work on your case. Some portions of every case can be handled by a competent paralegal under the supervision of an attorney, and this can save you money. Some clients may wish to spend most of their time with their attorney directly, though, seeking strategic planning and full discussion of all issues. On the other hand, some clients would rather keep billing to a minimum by spending most of their time with paralegals. Be sure to discuss your preference with your lawyer during the consultation. Listen to what the lawyer has to say. Determine if your goals are consistent. Be wary of any lawyer who tells you what you want without listening to you. Expect the lawyer to tell you exactly how he or she will try to get your case settled. Expect the lawyer to be candid about his or her family law experience and current case load. Experience is important because less-experienced lawyers may advise clients to take unrealistic positions or have expectations not based in reality. While no lawyer can predict the future, perspective and judgment comes from winning and also losing cases over a career.

Also, a lawyer with too many cases at one time can be as detrimental to your case as a lawyer who does not have enough experience. The most important factors to consider when hiring a lawyer are your confidence in the lawyer, experience, accessibility, responsiveness, compatibility, style, negotiating skills, reputation, and fees.

Expect a lawyer full of promises to be just that. Family law is rarely black and white. Leading you to believe a particular outcome is guaranteed can be downright irresponsible. While it is human nature to gravitate toward a more positive person, the most important part of being a lawyer is advising a client about the realities of a situation. The outcome of your divorce will almost always relate more to your ability to make smart decisions rather than the lawyer's courtroom skill. Smart decision making starts with understanding what can go wrong as well as what can go right, and a good attorney will help you understand this.

You should expect a clear picture of an attorney's billing and payment policies. The lawyer should detail the hourly rates of everyone in the office who will work on your case. Some lawyers may charge a flat fee. If so, be sure to understand exactly what the flat fee covers. You should learn how the lawyer charges for expenses such as photocopies, long-distance telephone calls, court reporters, and postage. Learn whether you are supposed to pay these expenses in advance. Different lawyers have different definitions of the word "retainer," so ask. Be concerned with the detailed nature of the billing statements or invoices. You should be able to clearly understand what work was performed and the length of time it took to complete the tasks.

Hourly rates and retainers vary greatly and depend on the lawyer's practice, case load, and popularity. If you ask experienced, professional family lawyers why divorces cost so much, they will tell you that it's due to revenge, pride, and fear on the part of one or both spouses. Aggrieved spouses seek revenge by directing their attorney to make the process as painful and expensive as possible. In other cases, a high price tag may be reasonable if one party has been denied access to the other's documents or accounts, causing costly discovery and motion practice. Some other estates are just plain complicated or include assets that are difficult to value such as closely held businesses or professional practices. Tell the lawyer what you can and cannot afford to pay. You should agree to receive legal services only if you'll be able to pay for them.

Tips for Keeping Legal Cost Down

Begin by learning about the divorce process. Learn the meaning of terms. Yes, there are legal terms and procedures a lawyer goes to law school to understand fully, but the more you yourself learn, the more informed your questions will be. Legal advice is a good thing, of course, because you need to know how Tennessee law applies to your situation. This knowledge will help you make more efficient use of your time with your lawyer. Ultimately, lawyers present you with options from which you must choose. Informed decision making will positively impact the quality of your life after divorce.

Complete the homework assigned by your lawyer in a timely fashion. "Homework" includes reading and learning about the divorce process, and it also means collecting and organizing the documents your lawyer needs early in a case. The more work you do organizing the documents and preparing information for your lawyer, the less the lawyer or paralegal must do. The faster you work, the faster your lawyer can take your work and do something with it. Always keep in mind that delay usually adds cost.

Carefully identify your most important strategic objectives and then share them with your lawyer. Together, pick your battles carefully. In family law, not every battle needs to be won or even fought. Scrutinize every issue before fighting over it. Some battles are worth fighting, but others just aren't. For example, you may choose to concede an issue and avoid going to court over $250 if it's going to cost you more than that just for your lawyer to drive to court and back. On the other hand, there are times that you need to send a message to your spouse that you are not afraid of the courthouse. Your strategic objectives should influence many of your decisions.

Lawyers and clients should create a "plan" together. If you don't know what the plan is, ask. Divorce is painful and complicated and can move quickly. Wrapping your head around everything can be tough. Clients can often forget the plan. If that happens, or if you think the lawyer has changed your plan, ask. As an analogy, think of driving to Kentucky with a friend and you see a sign that says, "Alabama—10 miles." You need to ask your driver, the lawyer, "Where are we going?" Be on the same page.

Batch your questions. In divorces, not every question must be answered that day. Get a notebook and write down your questions, save them, and make one call to your lawyer or paralegal. Often, asking several questions at a time can save a great deal of legal fees.

If you're upset over a particular issue, don't wait. Let your lawyer know you are upset and need your call returned. When you speak, stay on task, be direct, and get the answers you need. If your lawyer does not answer your questions or you didn't understand the answers, say so. If you are emotional, it would be better if you talked to a good friend or a mental health professional rather than your lawyer.

Read your invoices. Most family lawyers bill monthly. As soon as you receive an invoice for legal services, read it. Make sure you understand the billing descriptions. Write down questions. Never be afraid to ask your lawyer what was done or why some task was performed. Anyone can make a mistake in billing, even lawyers. But, don't wait to ask questions about billing. Memories fade with time.

When possible, avoid going to court to resolve disputed issues. Preparing for court can very expensive. Never use the threat to go to court to punish your spouse or to seek vindication. Keep your emotions in check. When you're too mad to talk to your spouse, just walk away. Call your lawyer and discuss options. Going to court should be a last resort.

Letting the other lawyer do all the work is a bad idea because the other lawyer is not looking out for you. Almost all divorce documents have subtle opportunities for the other lawyer to be an advocate for the other spouse, especially proposed settlement documents. Details matter. Letting the other lawyer do all the work could cost you in the long run.

Prepare a proposed settlement as soon as possible. For many reasons, including moving things along quicker, there may be negotiating advantages for having drafted the first settlement proposal to be shared with the other spouse. The main reason to draft it sooner is that it can settle the case! Even if you think it is a waste of time to draft a settlement because you firmly believe your spouse won't agree to it, it won't be a waste of time. Going through the process to draft a proposed settlement from start to finish will almost always ensure you and your lawyer on the same page. A settlement must be drafted eventually anyway, and sooner is usually better than later.

14
About the Author

Miles Mason, Sr. JD, CPA founded the Miles Mason Family Law Group, PLC, in Memphis, Tennessee, and serves clients in the Memphis area, including Germantown, Collierville, and counties throughout west Tennessee including Tipton and Fayette, and eastern Arkansas. The firm also handles select cases in Davidson and Williamson Counties, typically divorces including business valuations or forensic accounting investigations. For more information see www.MemphisDivorce.com.

The firm handles family law matters exclusively—divorce, child custody, child support, alimony modification, child support modification, prenuptial agreement litigation, and complex divorces involving business owners, business valuations, and forensic accounting issues.

Miles Mason, Sr., graduated from the University of Alabama in Tuscaloosa with a degree in accounting, became a CPA, practiced as an accountant, and returned to Memphis for law school. Along with Alan Crone, Miles cofounded Crone & Mason, PLC, and headed the firm's Family Law Practice Group for fifteen years. Then he formed the Miles Mason Family Law Group, PLC.

Miles Mason, Sr. has also authored *The Forensic Accounting Deskbook: A Practical Guide to Financial Investigation and Analysis for Family Lawyers*, published by the American Bar Association. *The Forensic Accounting Deskbook* is an easy-to-follow introduction to the world of forensic accounting and managing divorce litigation involving complex assets. To learn more about the book, visit www.ForensicAccountingDeskbook.com.

For the firm, leadership and service to the bar are priorities. Miles Mason, Sr., has served as Chair of the Tennessee Bar Association Family Law Section and has also served on the editorial board of the *Tennessee Bar Journal*. He is an active member of the American Bar Association's Family Law Section, having served on its CLE Committee and serving now as its Liaison to the AICPA (American Institute of Certified Public Accountants). Rated 10.0 out of 10.0 for family lawyers by Avvo.com, Miles is often interviewed by television and print news media for comment on Tennessee family law and legal stories.

As an additional service to the bar, Miles's speaking engagements center around sharing what he has learned about complex financial matters in divorce, forensic accounting, and business valuation. His national conference speaking engagements include the American Bar Association Family Law Section conferences, American Institute of CPAs National Business

Valuation Conference and National Forensic Accounting Conference, and the NACVA/IBA annual conferences. He also presents seminars for the Tennessee Bar Association, Tennessee Society of CPAs, Mississippi Society of CPAs, and other regional and local professional groups. Conference attendees include judges, lawyers, forensic accountants, business valuation experts, and psychologists in many cities across the country, including NYC, Boston, Chicago, LA, San Francisco, San Diego, Dallas, Denver, Orlando, and Las Vegas, in addition to Memphis, Nashville, Knoxville, and Chattanooga. Miles Mason has also authored articles for publications by the ABA Family Law Section's *Family Advocate*, the *Tennessee Bar Journal*, and the Georgia Bar Association Family Law Section. A complete list of speaking and publications are listed in his professional biography at MemphisDivorce.com.

The Miles Mason Family Law Group utilizes the team approach, bringing together very talented, dedicated, and compassionate attorneys and paralegals. Each professional focuses on what he or she does best. By working as a team and utilizing the latest technology to communicate, manage, and advance client matters, client interests are served more efficiently - always with an eye to resolving matters as quickly as possible. With financial expertise second to none, the firm handles simple and agreed-upon family law matters, as well as divorces involving complex estates with business valuations or requiring forensic accounting testimony.

Miles Mason, Sr. is also active in the community, having served on boards for several nonprofit organizations, including serving as President of the Christian Brothers High School Alumni Association; the Board of Directors of the Marguerite Piazza St. Jude Gala; and the Co-chair of the Board of Directors of the National Conference for Community and Justice (NCCJ). He resides in Memphis, Tennessee with his wife, Sharon, and their three children. For fun, Miles enjoys Alabama football, cycling, writing, shooting, and travel.

Bibliography and Resources

Barenbaum, Lester, Walter Schubert, and Robert Feder, *The Family Lawyer's Guide to Stock Options* (American Bar Association, Section of Family Law, 2007).

Carrad, David Clayton, *The Complete QDRO Handbook: Dividing ERISA, Military, and Civil Service Pensions and Collecting Child Support from Employee Benefit Plans,* 2d ed. (American Bar Association, Section of Family Law, 2004).

Hofheimer, Charles, *What Every Virginia Woman Should Know About Divorce* (Word Association Publishers, 2009).

Mason, Miles, *The Forensic Accounting Deskbook: A Practical Guide to Financial Investigation and Analysis for Family Lawyers* (American Bar Association, Section of Family Law, 2011).

Pratt, Shannon, *The Lawyer's Business Valuation Handbook: Understanding Financial Statements, Appraisal Reports, and Expert Testimony* (American Bar Association; Section of Family Law; General Practice, Solo and Small Firm Section; 2000).

Web Sites

www.MemphisDivorce.com: Detailed Tennessee family law information, advice, and resources and its Tennesse Family Law Blog

@Memphis_Divorce: Official Twitter account for Miles Mason Family Law Group, PLC

www.ABAnet.org/family/home.html, ABA Family Law Section

www.SupportGuidelines.com: Laura Morgan's Web site on all things related to child support

www.KBB.com: automobile resale values

www.csmonline.com: collectibles' values

www.Quote.com: stock quotes

www.SEC.gov: corporate information

www.BLS.gov: Bureau of Labor statistics

www.Child-abuse.com: Child abuse prevention network

Domestic Violence Resources:

Chattanooga
Partnership for Families, Children and Adults, (423) 755–2822

The Coalition Against Domestic and Community Violence of Greater Chattanooga, (423) 875–0120

Jackson
Women's Resource and Rape Assistance Program (WRAP)
(731) 668-0411
http://wraptn.org

Knoxville
Serenity Shelter
(865) 971–4673

Family Crisis Center
(865) 637–8000

Knoxville Police Department Domestic Violence Unit @ Knoxville
Family Justice Center
(865) 215–6810

Memphis
The Family Safety Center
www.familysafetycenter.org
(901) 222–4400

Sophia's House
www.accinwesttn.org
(901) 728–4229
(901) 722–4700

YWCA of Memphis
www.ymcamemphis.org
(901) 323–2211
(901) 725–4277 Crisis Hotline

Vday
www.vday.org
(212) 645–8329
(510) 841–4025

The Exchange Club Family Center
www.exchangeclub.net
(901) 726-2200

Nashville
YWCA—Nashville and Middle Tennessee
http://www.ywcanashville.com
(615) 269–9922
(615) 385–9754

Nashville Tennessee Baptist Healing Trust
www.baptisthealingtrust.org
(615) 284–8271

Tennessee Coalition Against Domestic and Sexual Violence
www.tcadsv.org
(615) 386–9406

National Resource Center for Domestic Violence:
(800) 537–2238
(800) 553–2508 (TTY)
nrcdvTA@nrcdv.org

National Domestic Violence Hotline (24 hour)
(800) 799–7233
(800) 787–3224 (TTY)

American Legion Family Support
Network Hotline (financial and family assistance)
(800) 504–4089
Online application at www.legion.org/fsn

Family Support Network
P.O. Box 1055
Indianapolis, IN 46206

Divorce Books for Children and Teens

Preschool:
Mom and Dad Don't Live Together Anymore. Stinson, Kathy (Annick Press, 1985).

Dinosaurs Divorce: A Guide for Changing Families. Brown, Laurene Kransy, and Brown, Marc (Boston: Little, Brown, 1986).

Five- to eight-year-olds:
All Kinds of Families. Simon, Norma (Albert Whitman, 2003).

All Families are Special. Simon, Norma (Albert Whitman, 1987).

Pre-teens:
Help! A Girl's Guide to Divorce and Stepfamilies. Holyoke, Nancy (Pleasant Co. Communications, 1999).

The Divorce Express. Danzinger, Paula (Delacorte, 1982).
Teens:
Divorce Handbook for Teens. MacGregor, Cynthia (Impact Publishers, 2004).

Divorce is not the End of the World. Stern, Zoe; Stern, Evan; Stern, Ellen Sue (Tricycle Press, 1997).

WA